LILI AT AYNHOE

Early nineteenth-century hand-coloured print of the south front of Aynhoe Park showing the house after Sir John Soane's alterations had been completed.

LILI AT AYNHOE

VICTORIAN LIFE
IN AN ENGLISH COUNTRY HOUSE

ELIZABETH
CARTWRIGHT-HIGNETT

BARRIE & JENKINS
LONDON

To J. and William, so they can remember too

First published in Great Britain in 1989 by
Barrie & Jenkins Ltd
289 Westbourne Grove, London W11 2QA

British Library Cataloguing in Publication Data
Cartwright-Hignett, Elizabeth
  Lili at Aynhoe: Victorian life in an English country house.
  1. England. Country houses. Social conditions, history
  I. Title
  942'.00880621
ISBN 0 7126 3520 3

Design by Behram Kapadia
Typeset by Wyvern Typesetting Ltd
Printed and bound in Portugal by Printer Portuguesa

Contents

Lady Elisabeth Cartwright, née von Sandizell, (1805–1902), known as Lili, and her husband
Sir Thomas Cartwright (1794–1850) of Aynhoe Park, Northamptonshire. Watercolour portraits
by Z. Grunbaum, painted in Munich in 1824.

Introduction

THE COUNTESS ELISABETH VON SANDIZELL, INVARIABLY known to her family as Lili, was my great-great-grandmother. I was named after her, a reflection on my parents' interest in this exotic Continental intruder into what had been hitherto a cheerfully xenophobic family of English country squires. So great was her influence on family attitudes that the next three generations married outside England, which produced a much more interesting spread of relatives for us.

Unlike Lili, my brother Edward and I were born at Aynhoe and I learned about her, as I grew up, from my parents and from the numerous objects connected with her which were around the house. Her paintings showed me what the rooms had looked like a hundred years or so earlier, with so many of the contents still there and used by us every day. I read the snippets from her diary which had been translated from the original French, but it was not until many years later that I attempted to grapple with the remainder of it and by that time we were no longer living at Aynhoe. The idea that one day I might be able to write a book about her, using her diary and her paintings, always remained with me. However, it did not turn out to be quite what I had expected.

For anyone brought up in one of the larger country houses, the experience is a dominating one. Although we were quite unselfconscious about our surroundings as children, taking them for granted and enjoying the freedom that they gave us, a sense of history and continuity gradually infiltrated from constant exposure to our ancestors and their works. Other centuries seemed quite as real to us as the international events reported by the newspapers and the radio. Not only the huge house but the landscape itself had been changed by our forebears. So much in our lives was centred on Aynhoe, its past and its future, and above all the perpetual struggle of the present to keep the place going.

My brother and I spent the war years in America with our Nanny, and we came back to Aynhoe in the winter of 1945. I was just six when we returned and Edward was eight. The house was occupied by the Army and the park was still one of the biggest petrol stores in the Midlands. By that summer, Italian prisoners of war were removing Nissen huts and clearing concrete from the park and the gardens, but it took several years for our parents to repair the damage.

When the Army had left, the house was redecorated as much as limited cash and the shortage of materials would allow, and the furniture, which had been stored in the orangery, the salon and the old kitchen, was replaced in the rooms. Largely owing to my mother's enterprise, the house was opened to the public in 1950, being among one of the first groups of houses to do so. The visitors came with the daffodils each year and departed at the end of the harvest throughout my childhood. Petrol shortages ensured that we spent most of our time at Aynhoe and, assisted by bicycles, we ran wild there during the curious period of peace following a world convulsion that had been even more terrible than the Napoleonic wars of which Lili must have been aware in her own childhood.

Aynhoe Park stands on the edge of the village of Aynho, a pretty settlement of yellow-grey limestone houses. It is situated in the southernmost corner of Northamptonshire between Banbury and Bices-

Pencil sketch of a bridge near Aynhoe by Lili, from her sketch book of 1828.

ter, on a hill overlooking the edge of the Cotswolds. The 'Great House' lies close to the road in the south-western corner of the village, but any attempt to admire it from a car is fraught with risk as it is adjacent to a wicked corner created by the consummation of the desire of William Ralph Cartwright, Lili's father-in-law, to extend his park. Many of the houses in the village have apricot trees planted on their walls, a unique feature which is generally thought, incorrectly, to have been due to a traditional part-payment of rent in apricots. In fact, the origin of this custom is unknown, but the result is charming. The difference in the spelling of the house and the village results from the desire of some member of the Cartwright family in the nineteenth century to stick to the supposedly more authentic version when the Post Office wished to modernize it.

Lacemakers at Aynhoe, outside their cottage, 1816. Lili mentions in her diary in 1845 that the lace of Aynhoe and its neighbourhood is 'not what it was in earlier times; the good workers are found now on the other side of the county'.

Originally a medium-sized manor house with a series of medieval absentee landlords, Aynhoe was acquired in 1615 along with a substantial estate by Richard Cartwright, a successful lawyer. His father had been a yeoman sheep farmer in Cheshire.

The house was burnt out by the defeated Royalist forces who had occupied it during the Civil War, while its owner, Richard's grandson John, who was a Parliamentarian, had wisely retired to London before they arrived. He had previously been attainted for treason. This appears to have been as much for his marital behaviour as for his politics, since he had locked up his erring wife in a farmhouse before the war. Her family, the Noys, had powerful influence at Court, and when persuasion failed to release her, they pressed for stronger measures to be taken. This was made easier when he refused to pay the Ship Money tax introduced by his father-in-law. Some years after the war ended, the house was rebuilt within the original shell but in a more classical style.

By the beginning of the eighteenth century the estate had recovered from the devastation of the Civil War. John's grandson, the first Thomas Cartwright (his son William of Bloxham having pre-deceased him), had ample resources to enable him to extend the house using, it is thought, the designs of Thomas Archer carried out by his own master mason, Edward Wing, and supervised by himself. This he did with gusto, lengthening the central block to the east and the west and adding two independent staff and stable blocks on the village side. He was then able to settle down to plant up his newly-enclosed park, create a formal garden and enjoy country politics and pleasures in rustic grandeur.

His son, the second William, and his grandson, the second Thomas, followed his lead, consolidating the estate and taking their turns as Members of Parliament and Justices of the Peace. This Thomas died relatively young, and his son, William Ralph Cartwright, inherited Aynhoe when he was a baby. Fortunately for him, his stepfather administered the estate with wisdom and foresight, with the result that by the time he came of age, in 1792, he was a very wealthy young man. His ideas expanded by a Grand Tour which included a visit to St Petersburg, he felt that his home was somewhat old-fashioned and inconvenient as it had been little changed since his great-grandfather's time. He invited Sir John Soane to alter it. A number of different plans were produced which resulted in changes to the exterior. These included the creation of arches linking the wings to the central block. Pediments were built on to the top of the main block, front and back, and were removed from the library and conservatory. Soane put them on the east and west ends instead. Having shuffled the pediments about to his satisfaction, he set about remodelling the interior.

Plans for a ballroom, a great double staircase and an exotic painted vestibule were abandoned owing to a shortage of funds, but the main suite of rooms, the servants' quarters and service areas and a few of the bedrooms were completely remodelled. Externally, the house remains virtually unchanged since that time. The interior of the house gives an

Wash drawing by Lili of the south front of Aynhoe viewed from half way down the park, showing part of the avenue of elm trees planted by Thomas Cartwright in the first decade of the eighteenth century.

impression of light and space. The rooms are very large, but in proportion to the scale of the building. Their design is neither overwhelmingly grand nor too severe, a state brought about as much by the lack of money as by the taste of Soane and his client, but the prevailing opinion of the time was that it was friendly, elegant and extremely comfortable.

For us, the winter at Aynhoe was very quiet, and much less social than in Lili's time, but we were more used to country activities and the climate than she was. When she knew it, the house was warm owing to the activities of a large staff. In my childhood, for reasons of economy and a primitive central heating system which only warmed the air to six inches above the few radiators in the passages, the house was bitterly cold and the wind used to howl inside the cavity walls. There were arctic spaces to be crossed in my vast bedroom from the bed to the single-bar

A cottage in Aynhoe by Lili, 1828. Like many village houses at that time it was semi-ruinous, the walls crumbling and the thatch missing in places.

electric heater. Lili knew the house when every room was used, at the height of its prosperity. In our day, in straitened circumstances but surrounded by beautiful things, we lived in the middle floor of the middle block and there were rarely more than two flats occupied in the whole of the rest of the house. There were ghostly deserts of empty rooms which I had to dare myself to explore on my own. The walls of the wings, last occupied by the Army, were covered with drawings of Mr Chad and with graffiti which I was too young to understand. It was an immensely exciting place for a child, and I loved it.

In 1954 my father and brother were killed in a car accident. The estate was left with a similar set of problems to those which had obtained after Lili's father-in-law, William Ralph Cartwright, died in 1847. This time it was not possible to hang on and wait for better times, as Lili's son had done, and we sold Aynhoe in 1960 with a great sense of regret but also of necessity. The family had been there for over three hundred years, father to son, and each generation had loved it and struggled with its problems – from mortgages to dry rot – as we did. Aynhoe is now the property of the Country Households Association and as full of interested people as it was in the middle of the nineteenth century. To have spent such an important period of my life there was a great privilege, despite the difficulties with which my parents, far more than myself, had to contend.

When I started to write this book, I intended it to be a straight-forward description of the house and the rooms shown in Lili's paintings, reinforced by selections from her diary showing the life of the household at the time. However, so vivid were my memories of a childhood happily spent in the same place, among many objects that are still with us, and so great was the sense of continuity within the family, that my own experiences kept finding their way into the text. Its purpose has been, perhaps, to revive some of the ghosts of the nineteenth century and to come to terms, most enjoyably, with some of my own.

Lili and the Family

I N 1828 A YOUNG GERMAN WOMAN VISITED AYNHOE PARK FOR THE first time. Living in Munich with her husband of three years, she had yet to meet her family or set eyes on their huge country house about which she had heard so much. Arriving with her were her husband and small son, the future heirs to the estate. She was fully aware of the importance of this visit and of how much many relationships within the family in the future would depend on its success.

Later in her married life, Lili was to spend long months at Aynhoe without her husband. In the interminable intervals between the dispatch of her letters and the receipt of his, she confided her thoughts to her diary and occupied many empty or troubled hours with making paintings of the interior of the house, which she had come to love. Lili's paintings and her diary have been a source of much entertainment and interest within the family ever since. Others of her generation at Aynhoe spent their evenings compiling scrapbooks and prevailing upon their numerous guests to contribute something original to them. Taken together they make up a fascinating record of life in an English country house in the years surrounding Queen Victoria's accession to the throne.

Lili was born in 1805, the eldest daughter of Count Thomas von Sandizell, a Bavarian nobleman. He was the Grand Master to the Duchess of Zweibrücken, a Princess Royal of Saxony, at Neuburg. She was brought up at the family home of Schloss Sandizell, a vast mansion surrounded by a moat between the Danube marshes and the great forests north of Munich, and educated at the Maison Royale, a boarding school for daughters of the nobility, which had been initiated by King Max-

Portrait of Lili's father, Count Thomas von Sandizell, taken from a piece of Nymphenburg porcelain. This was one of a series of portrait cups produced by this factory and depicting eminent persons at the Bavarian court.

imilian Joseph in 1813, the year in which she entered it at seven years old. This school was based on the Maison d'Ecouen, the boarding school for young ladies which Napoleon had founded in France a year or two before. At this time, Bavaria was at peace with Napoleon and the Monarchy was supported by him. Lili left school when she was seventeen in 1823, having remained within its boundaries for ten years, except for one weekend when she went to the funeral of her grandmother, Countess Törring-Gutenzell.

Lili's maternal grandfather had been the Chief Minister to King Maximilian of Bavaria and to his two predecessors, but he had been sacked on the accession of King Ludwig. Nevertheless Lili was familiar with Court circles and was something of a favourite with the Queen. On leaving school she was presented at Court and for the next eighteen months led a very active social life in one of the most brilliant Courts in Europe. Lili was tiny (in 1834 she weighed six and a half stone), fair-haired and pretty, as her portrait shows. She was observant and intelligent, with strong and informed opinions of her own, but this was offset by her training in female compliance, so typical of the period. Later on she wrote of her experiences of this time with vividness and humour.

In 1824 she met a young English diplomat, Thomas Cartwright, during the Munich Carnival. Thomas was Secretary to the English Legation and showed every sign of embarking on a distinguished diplomatic career. He was the eldest son of a family of thirteen. A handsome man with dark curly hair, he was hot-tempered, intelligent and energetic. He loved music and intellectual pursuits but was inclined to cut a dash and as a result tended towards extravagance. Some time later, Lili described how he had just bought the 'finest pair of carriage horses in Frankfurt'. He was a keen shot, like most of the men in his family, and during his lifetime managed to enjoy this activity from the

LILI'S INTRODUCTION TO HER DIARY, 1828

He was the eldest son of a Mr. Cartwright, Member of Parliament for the County of Northamptonshire, and he was Secretary to the English Legation in Munich. We met nearly every day at the different parties which were given during Carnival and we talked a great deal. I found him very pleasant. I was far from believing or imagining that he thought to marry me. He spoke to Papa and received a favourable response. I was very surprised when Mama asked for my views but I gave my consent without hesitation and I have never regretted the choice that I made.

William Ralph Cartwright MP in the library, aged about forty. Coloured drawing by Edridge. This was one of several Edridge portraits of members of the family, one of which portrayed William Ralph's wife Julia and their son Henry and which can be seen in Lili's picture of Julia's sitting room.

Alps (chamois in Bavaria) to the North Sea (duck in Belgium). Above all, however, he was dedicated to his work and to Aynhoe, his family home.

William Ralph Cartwright, Thomas's father, was the archetypal Tory squire of the period, conservative in his views, rooted in his own area, a supporter of Church and Monarchy and with a profound mistrust of the Irish, foreigners and the Pope. It was something of a shock, therefore, when Thomas wrote home to tell his father of his intention to marry Lili, who was not only Bavarian, from a country with a monarchy set up by the infamous Napoleon (against whom his second son William had risked his life at Waterloo), but who was also a Catholic. William Ralph objected to the marriage, threatening not to receive Lili, but Thomas, who was a determined character, went home to confront his father on the matter and somehow the objections were overcome. Lili's father also objected to her marriage to a foreign Protestant, but his attitude changed fairly rapidly when permission for the marriage was granted by the Pope, and when he considered that he had two more unmarried daughters, for whom dowries might have to be provided, while Thomas, being English, seems not to have demanded one. Their wedding took place in 1824 in the Bishop's chapel at Augsburg with few, if any, of the Cartwright family present.

For the next few years they lived in Munich, where their first son, Willy, was born. In due course, Thomas decided that it was time to present his wife and son to his family, so they set off on the long journey to England and to Aynhoe.

Lili began to write a diary in 1828, an astonishing document which she kept up to the end of her long life. This diary has been the prime source of information on her paintings and on the activities of the family at that period. She wrote it, surprisingly, in French, perhaps to prevent the German or English servants from reading it. She was an acute observer of character and very broad-minded for someone of her upbringing over the eccentricities of human nature. Her strictures on the behaviour of others are reserved for those who appeared to be failing in what she felt was their familial duty. She shows an open and enquiring mind although the focus of her loyalty and activity lay within the family. She was a perceptive observer of the political scene, both in England and on the Continent, and she was warm-hearted and lively,

LILI'S INTRODUCTION, 1828

I was enchanted with everything, and above all with Mrs. Cartwright. She is the second wife of my father-in-law, who lives with her in perfect happiness. She brings up all the children with extreme care and loves them all as if they were her own. To all the qualities of the heart she adds those of the mind. She is well educated, of a charming gaiety and always of an equable temper.

On her first visit to England with her husband Thomas in 1828, Lili drew their house in Munich from memory to show the family where they lived. Her early efforts at drawing make it look like a doll's house.

enjoying the social activities required of her position as the wife of a rising diplomat. Her diary records the everyday events that one would expect, but also the diplomatic activities and preoccupations of her husband and his family, with comments of her own which show her independent views. Lili often disagreed with her father-in-law's convictions from her more sophisticated Continental background. Perhaps the only person she might have been able to share her opinions with was her husband, and during her later visits to Aynhoe he was frequently not there.

Of William Ralph's large family only his eldest daughter, Emma, had not survived. His first wife had been Emma Maude, daughter of the first Lord Hawarden and relative of the renowned Ralph Allen of Bath. They had eight children: Emma, Thomas, William, Mary, Cornwallis, Robert, Stephen and Sophie. Several of them were born in Bath during the period when Aynhoe was being remodelled. Their mother died, exhausted, perhaps, by the rapid arrival of so many children. In 1810, William Ralph married his second wife, Julia Aubrey, the daughter of a Welsh squire. They had five children: Richard Aubrey, Henry, Fanny,

Pair of watercolour portraits by Richmond of Fanny (who married Matthew Boulton) and Julia
(who married the Rev. Edward Goulbourn), the youngest daughters of William Ralph
and Julia Cartwright.

Julia and Freddy. Not surprisingly, Lili found her first meeting with the family more than a little daunting.

As always, her diary keeps us in touch with her experiences. But William Ralph had recently voted, typically, against Catholic emancipation and on her feelings towards him she observes an eloquent silence. (Indeed throughout her times at Aynhoe Lili must have exercised a great deal of tact and forbearance over questions of religion.) About her mother-in-law she had no such reservations. Her praise was undoubtedly sincere since she was more than capable of blunt comment in her private writings when she chose to be.

More liberal in attitude than William Ralph, Thomas found his career was sometimes hampered by his father's long association with the Tory party. As a diplomat he was passed over by the Tory administration for a post in Paris, which he merited by his ability, on the grounds that he was not enough of a party man, yet he did not fare very well under a Whig government because of his father's views.

At this time, William Ralph was a busy Member of Parliament for South Northamptonshire, father of thirteen children, and owner of an enormous house which had cost a great deal to refurbish and which was now permanently full to the roof with family and friends. It required, at least in his view, an indoor staff of twenty-two to run it. He entertained on the grand scale, and much money was spent on obtaining political support in the area. Added to this, the price of farm produce fell as soon as the war with Napoleon was over, greatly impoverishing the estate and reducing the rents. Not surprisingly there was a financial crisis. Fortunately he was saved from the consequences of this by the timely demise of a relative who left him all her money. This enabled him to pay off the kind of overdraft at which even a modern estate owner would have hesitated and to continue to live in the same lavish manner as before. While he staved off the immediate catastrophe, his life-style made financial difficulties for the next generation inevitable, and gave only small allowances for his huge family as they grew up.

Lily's next visit to Aynhoe was in 1834, six years later. This time she and her younger son Tommy, who was four years old, travelled on their own. Thomas was unable to join her for some months owing to his work and he stayed behind with their older son, Willy. By this time, Thomas had been posted to Brussels, from where he had been caught up in the

Colonel William
Cartwright, Thomas's
closest brother, a
watercolour portrait by
Josiah Dighton, who
painted a series of informal
pictures of all those in the
family who were available
to sit for him at Aynhoe
around 1840.

siege of Antwerp and was now dealing with the diplomatic aftermath. Lili was anxious about going to England without him but there was the hope that he would join her in a month or so.

At Aynhoe, Lili found that all the family had grown up, except Freddy who was at Eton. Fanny and Julia, the youngest daughters, still occupied the schoolroom as their special domain although they were of marriageable age, and the rest of the family were frequently in the house as most of them lived in the district. William Ralph was involved with an election, so there were many visits from his political cronies to shoot and to dine.

After some months, Lili's initial pleasure at seeing all her husband's family again and her excitement in rediscovering Aynhoe became somewhat diminished. She missed her husband and Willy and her diary is full of references to her loneliness and the dampness of the British winter compared to that of Bavaria (and the extent to which the English moaned about it themselves) and the sheer monotony of country life, especially in the evenings. She disliked what social events there were, such as the balls which were held locally. This is hardly surprising in view of her sense of isolation and the very different social scene, of receptions and assemblies in one of the most brilliant Courts in Europe, with which she was familiar. Delightful as the country might have seemed at first, now she was bored and she longed for her husband and elder son and to be mistress in her own house. To occupy the time that hung so heavily on her hands, she decided to start a series of watercolours of the interior of the house.

Like most young ladies, she had been taught to draw at school but had not shown any unusual talent. On her previous visit to Aynhoe she had done a few drawings, some of which found their way into various scrapbooks. They were rather stiff and simple, but one album shows her determination to practise and improve. She copied masterpieces in museums, studied prints and drew scenes in the countryside. By the time of her return to Aynhoe in 1834, she was more confident of her ability. So enthusiastic was she, that soon she had taught her mother-in-law, Julia, to do the same. They painted together on many occasions and Julia, too, embarked on a long series of interiors, of Aynhoe and of many other houses, and these pictures, like Lili's, are still in the possession of the family. Both became highly competent in time, although Lili's pictures have greater quality and are outstanding for an amateur. Other

LILI'S INTRODUCTION, 1828

Their dinners are very long and boring, their assemblies very much too full of people to enjoy the charms of conversation and their dances are the saddest things. No sentiments of gaiety animate them. They dance mechanically, like automata, and one sees a little smile of satisfaction begin on their lips the moment the carriages are announced. To amuse oneself in England, one must stay in the country where life is spent delightfully.

5 DECEMBER 1834

Julia and I went to one of the villagers' houses in Aynhoe and drew the interior. The weather was delightful.

members of the family were similarly gifted and their work has been preserved in their scrapbooks: some of their sketches, or those of their guests, showing their pets, their portraits of each other, hunting scenes and family parties, are reproduced here.

Lili's paintings began in December and they continued until she left in May the following year. While it is clear from her diary that she took a lively and intelligent interest in all that went on around her – and in an election year that meant many political visitors and discussions at Aynhoe – as a woman and a foreigner she would have found that her views, however well informed, were not highly regarded. The plaintive note that sometimes creeps into her diary entries is an indication that, as the long winter wore on, Lili came to rely more and more on her writing and painting, both as a means of passing her time and as a channel for her remarkable energies and curiosity.

The west end of the house; watercolour by Julia from her album of interiors showing the high arched windows of the library and her own sitting room windows above looking out over the small parterre and terrace.

THE NORTH FRONT, DECEMBER 1834

Lili's Paintings

1834– 35

THE NORTH FRONT   DECEMBER 1834

L ILI'S PAINTING OF AYNHOE'S NORTH FRONT SHOWS THE HOUSE
as she had first seen it six years previously, and the first view she
had of her destination when she arrived once again in October
1834 after an unpleasant sea crossing.

Her picture shows the central block of the house as it was rebuilt after
the Civil War. The principal entrance as shown is probably contemporary with that rebuild, but it would have been the back door at the time as
the main façade faced to the south over the park. In 1707, the wings to
right and left in the picture were added to Archer's design for the first
Thomas Cartwright, although they were then detached from the house.
The north elevation of the main block was altered to match the new
wings, and on the south front the library and conservatory extensions
were built. The latter, along with Thomas Cartwright's newly-planted
trees in the park, can be seen in a drawing by Tillemans in the British
Museum.

The final changes to the house took place around 1802, when Sir
John Soane completed his alterations for Lili's father-in-law William
Ralph. These included the creation of arches which linked the wings to
the main block, and the dome over the stairs which looks slightly like a
birdcage in Lili's painting. This was one of Lili's first attempts at painting
and it is clear that she was in difficulties with perspective. The shape and
size of the dome over the stairs is largely a product of her imagination
since it can scarcely be seen from there, even without the shrubbery.

The wing on the left was the stable block. The haylofts and the
grooms' accommodation were on the upper floors and William Ralph's

12 OCTOBER 1834

*On Tuesday at four o'clock,
while we were at dinner on
board the* Batavia, *the vessel ran
aground on a sandbank from
which we were pulled by two
gunboats but not before seven
on the Friday evening. Days
spent in such a manner are not
agreeable, especially in a Dutch
vessel where the Captain is idle
and where everything is badly
designed. We were happy
enough with the company and
amongst the 75 passengers I
found several who were very
pleasant. All my discomforts
vanished from my mind when I
saw the banks of the Thames
and the Port of London where
we arrived on Saturday at
midday.*

8 DECEMBER 1834

*While coming from Astrop,
where the roads are
abominable, one of the post
horses fell and, in the process,
brought down the other horse
and the postillion. Thus you
have the consequences of the
bad road from Astrop.*

coachman had a flat there. The last two windows close to the arch were the windows of the harness room, with its snug fireplace and smells of leather, Stockholm tar and neat's-foot oil. When Lili was at Aynhoe the stables must have been even more full of horses than they were during my adolescence (I shared the stables with a friend), but when I knew it the rest of the wing was empty. It was haunted by strange noises and occasionally our horses would take fright for no apparent reason. Lili was not a horsewoman and was not too keen on carriages either, being acquainted with their unreliability. She recorded that she and her husband had an eccentric coachman in Munich called Cockle, who used to drive with his wheels as close to the ditch as possible in order to demonstrate his skill. She was also carriage-sick (an unexpected hazard of the pre-motor era) and described an occasion when they all went from Aynhoe to a ball at Woodstock, some twelve miles away. She was very sick throughout the evening, but had to go on dancing all night.

The arch on the left led through to the carriage house, now a garage, via an architecturally confused gap between the wing and the central block. It was here that Soane had intended a ballroom to be built, before the funds ran out. The arch on the right contains the housekeeper's room, which Lili illustrated some years later, and it is attached to the staff wing on the western side of the house which held the kitchen, the laundry and other domestic offices. The staff accommodation was above.

8 DECEMBER 1834

*Aynhoe has been very busy
today. Preparations were being
made to receive Sir Charles
Knightley who came to dinner
and to spend the night here.
One sees on every side flags of
the Knightley colours, blue and
violet. The horses wore blue
cockades; the bells rang; music
took place on the terrace and
was played during the whole
evening; toasts were given; the
servants danced and altogether
there were endless rejoicings
and very tedious they were.*

THE SOUTH FRONT   DECEMBER 1834

AYNHOE WAS A CENTRE OF GREAT POLITICAL EXCITEMENT DURING THE autumn in which Lili arrived. Her diary is full of descriptions of the activities of the household. There were numerous visitors and visits to neighbours; the men hunted and shot and there was much electoral activity which she recorded with relish. Her father-in-law had been returned as the member for South Northamptonshire in 1832, as had

THE SOUTH FRONT, DECEMBER 1834

6 JANUARY 1835

I was in Banbury with Robert to make some purchases. We found the town so quiet that it might have been in mourning, for the election had taken place. Mr. Lloyd Williams, sure of the result and surrounded by his friends, sent himself about a plan of campaign. I do not know what evil spirit possessed him, but he read such an ultra-Tory speech that the inhabitants of Banbury, who had only recently given up Radicalism, left him because of his policies and voted for Mr. Tancred, and so all have become Radicals through the bad judgement of Mr. Lloyd Williams. The latter has fallen ill with the chagrin of not being elected.

Lord Althorp who stood for the Whigs, when a compromise had been reached between the parties for one Whig and one Tory to stand in each of the two divisions of the county. Lord Althorp and his Whig allies had earlier defeated William Ralph over the Reform Bill controversy. On Althorp's elevation to the Spencer earldom, and so to the House of Lords, Lili notes that there was no Whig candidate to take his place and Sir Charles Knightley had a chance to re-enter politics as member for North Northamptonshire. He was a regular visitor to Aynhoe, his family home being at Fawsley some twenty miles away. A popular landowner of ultra-conservative views, he was a great rider to hounds and had a famous herd of shorthorns. Lili's description of him suggests that she felt he rather resembled them in character. This painting shows the terrace where the celebrations for Sir Charles's political victory took place.

The boundary of the original house is visible, with the wings added on in 1707. These were increased in height and had the upper windows added by Soane. The conservatory takes up the whole of the right-hand wing and the left contains the vestibule and library on the ground floor and the sitting room and main bedroom above. The central window on the ground floor was the front door of the original house, and the façade is much as it was when rebuilt after the Civil War. Lili's picture, however, does not show the tops of the cellar windows, which date from that time or earlier. I long to know who were the two children she shows on the terrace. The little girl has a poke bonnet and the boy a top hat.

As children we had the big room in the centre of the house on the first floor as our playroom. Curiously enough, it was dark and gloomy despite its two large windows. We did our best, accidentally, to set the house on fire one wet day when we let off an unauthorized firework from the central window ledge. A gust of wind blew it back into the corner of a broken window sash and a quantity of decorative sparks disappeared up inside it. We poured water on the bottom of the sash and then, horrified, waited until clouds of smoke started to pour out of the top of the window before we went for help. The fire appeared to be out but it restarted a few hours later and it was necessary to expose a lot of brickwork under the shutters and the plaster in order to suppress it finally. We were not very popular with my mother, but my father may have enjoyed the excitement in retrospect, since he had organized the Aynho Fire Brigade in previous years and regular practice drill would take place on the lawn in

8 DECEMBER 1834

Sir Charles Knightley is one of those violent Tories who are anti-Catholic and who I am not pleased to see. If I had a vote to give, it would not be he to whom I gave it. He is violent beyond the limit of good sense. He is fanatical on the subject of politics. The continual attacks in bad taste, and directed personally against Whigs, have even disgusted some Tories.

between bouts of extinguishing thatch and haystack fires. The Fire Brigade came to an unfortunate end when the woodshed in the timber yard in the middle of the village went on fire, reducing the fire engine and the only hydrant, which were kept there, to ashes, while the village and its Fire Brigade watched. The carriage in which Lord Nelson had travelled to sign the Treaty of Copenhagen was incinerated at the same time, though how it came to be there no one seems to remember.

In front of the lawn is the ha-ha, dividing the garden from the park. It is six feet six inches high but it never seemed to stop the deer in the park from leaping up it in order to eat the wallflowers lovingly provided by our gardener, Ted Humphris, for the delight of the public when the house was open. In the autumn we could watch from our playroom window the bucks fighting with locked antlers, backing away and hurling themselves at each other again with a crash. When the grass was less sweet in winter, the deer would stand on their hind legs and reach up to nibble the shoots of the cedar trees.

To the right of the house can be seen the tower of the church. In Lili's day the rest of the family and household were regular churchgoers, although she describes visiting, when she could, the little Catholic church at Hethe, some six miles away.

25 DECEMBER 1834

I left at nine o'clock to go to Hethe this morning where I arrived at ten and attended Divine Service. I was very happy to hear Mass and to worship the Lord in a Church. I returned here at one o'clock.

THE SALON   DECEMBER 1834

AFTER THE ELECTION OF SIR CHARLES KNIGHTLEY, THE political activity in the household settled down for a while. The bad weather was giving Lili more opportunity to paint and to take time to observe the details of the rooms. It had the added advantage of enabling her to escape from the other guests.

In her painting of the salon, the conservatory doors at the far end of the room are closed, and vague vegetable shapes can be seen through them. A big room, the salon has pictures which are in proportion in size and attitude. On the left is a rather overblown painting of the Repentant

4 DECEMBER 1834

I have set myself to do some drawing, and want to begin some interiors of rooms.

THE SALON, DECEMBER 1834

Magdalene in the style of Guido Reni. The painting over the fireplace is unidentifiable but the next three are by Murillo. *St Anthony with the Christ Child* now hangs in the Barber Institute in Birmingham and *The Assumption of the Madonna* is in the Fort Worth Museum in Texas. The portraits of a Dutch couple between the windows are probably from the studio of Rubens: the wife always looks to me as if she had a particularly bad cold.

This is the first of the main rooms painted by Lili to have a fitted carpet. The walls are painted a rather unusual dark grey which complements the pink-striped upholstery. The curtains, bunched up so that they do not reach the floor until they are pulled across, are in a dark pink heavy velvet with light lace curtains behind. There are gold rope tie-backs and a gold fringe on the pelmets. The decor seems to have been carefully thought out and all of one period. This would probably have been some thirty years previously, after Soane renovated the house, but since he did little or nothing to alter this room architecturally it remained much as it had been in 1707 in that respect.

The pair of elegant side tables between the windows is still with us and is from the previous century. Lili's painting makes them look immensely tall compared to the nearby sofa table. They have been backed with the same striped material as the chairs. The sofa table, with its green baize top, is used as a writing table and she shows the inkstand with its pen and blotter. Was this the table at which she sat to write her long and wistful letters to her husband in Frankfurt, hoping for his return?

There are two plant stands in the room and several more in the other main rooms. I think the plants are hyacinths (from the greenhouses that she illustrates later) but it is difficult to be sure. Someone has lovingly made a panel of tapestry work for the cushion at the back of the chair by the fire, and there are books and a workbox on the tables. Several of the smaller pieces of furniture are still with us, but not the chairs or the sofas. I remember as a child seeing the splendid square love-seat stored after the war in the old kitchen and looking very dilapidated before it was finally sold.

The three great vases, two on the side tables and one in the corner on a pillar, are protected from accidental damage by gold cords to stop them being knocked over. As in the other rooms there are numerous small

28 DECEMBER 1834

I spent Sunday as usual. I wrote a great deal; writing letters is a great comfort and consolation when one finds oneself far from one's own . . .

24 DECEMBER 1834

I spent the morning drawing; the festival of Christmas has not occupied me this year, since this festival is not celebrated in England as it is at home in Germany.

objects of china and glass (mostly impossible to identify) and bronzes on the mantelpiece. These consist of two jugs and four figures, the end figures supporting ormolu candelabra. The room looks comfortable and well used, but more formal than the Soane drawing room next door.

THE FRONT HALL   30 DECEMBER 1834

CHRISTMAS HAD BEEN DULL FOR LILI, THOUGH THE HOUSE had been full of visitors whose hats and galoshes stood ever ready in the front hall.

The front hall lies in the centre of the main house, facing north towards the village. For such an imposing building Aynhoe has an unenterprising front entrance, inside and out. Neither Archer nor Soane, in their alterations, managed to make much out of it. In Lili's painting the front door, such as it is, is completely hidden and masquerades as the central window. Inner doors, designed to minimize the tremendous draughts, have been pushed back to the walls on either side with coconut matting in front of them. The draught-excluding red baize door at the far end of the room has long since disappeared.

The hall remains much as Soane left it, after he had enlarged it at either end and added the sets of twin pillars so typical of his work. The cornice appears to have been from the time of Archer's rebuild. Soane's plans for a grand double staircase here having been frustrated for lack of funds, he also seems to have forgotten to do anything interesting to the fireplace, which is a miserable little affair in the context of the scale and grandeur of the room. This seems to have replaced an exotic creation in the William Kent style full of blackened carved wood figures and swags of fruit. All that remains of this now are two worm-eaten but voluptuous caryatids who stand on a bath in our house and whose breasts have achieved a high polish from passing decorators and plumbers. My grandfather, Sir Fairfax Cartwright, disliked the fireplace shown in Lili's picture. He and his Italian wife had one made to their design when he

31 DECEMBER 1834

We were twenty to dinner today and celebrated the end and the beginning of the year with numerous entertainments, mine being more absurd and misplaced than the others. My heart was full; I thought of my husband and of Willy and I would have preferred only to go back to my own home.

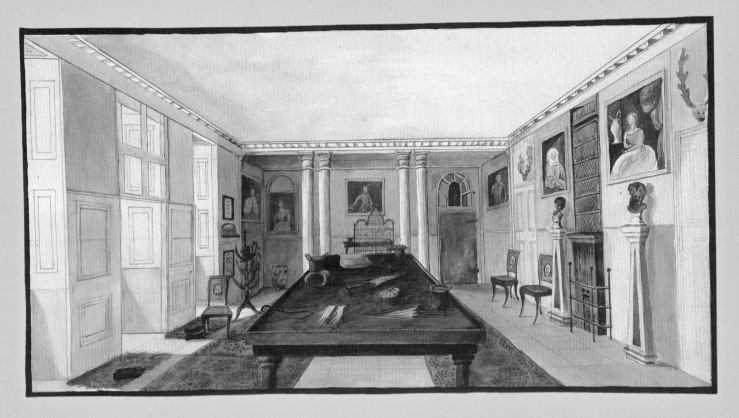

THE FRONT HALL, 30 DECEMBER 1834

was in post at the British Legation in Mexico in 1902. It is carved from one of the largest pieces of pale green Mexican onyx ever found and the work was carried out by an Italian craftsman, Francesco Laffi, who was working in Mexico at the time.

Lili's perspective, like the fireplace and front door, shows signs of strain in living up to the task required of it. These were early days in her series of interiors, and the backs of many of the leaves in her sketchbooks show her practice attempts at perspective drawing. However, her sense of detail was becoming apparent. She shows various items on the baize-covered table – gloves, two umbrellas, four top hats, a cap, a shooting bag and what may be a hunting whip. There are two pairs of galoshes near the front door, one of them probably her own, a hat on the table at the far end of the hall, and another top hat on a peculiar-looking hatstand which seems to imitate the antlers of the fallow bucks from the park, souvenirs from previous shooting expeditions, hanging on the opposite wall. A similar buck from the same period regards us morosely from the bottom of our stairs. The number and type of objects in the hall must have varied with the fluctuating inhabitants over the Christmas period. Lili had felt very lonely, despite the activity.

The hall is relatively sparsely furnished compared to other rooms. She shows in detail the splendid set of chairs designed by Soane for the house, with their curved backs and scimitar legs. The Cartwright crest is painted on the back. These chairs are still in the family, as slippery and uncomfortable now as they were then. The two marble stands are still at Aynhoe.

The portraits are as follows, from left to right: Nathaniel, Lord Crewe, by Sir Godfrey Kneller. He was the Bishop of Durham in the time of James II. Next is Byzantia Cartwright, probably by Hudson, then Sir Clement Cotterell, wearing the Seal of Lord High Chamberlain, a hereditary post in his family. The second William Cartwright, son of the first Thomas, hangs in the corner, and on either side of the fireplace are the first William Cartwright and his wife, Ursula Fairfax, who was the sister of the Civil War general, both by Lely.

The floor is stone-flagged and has two runners. In our time the flags were bare, which my brother and I found convenient. On wet days we used to roller-skate from the oak staircase beyond the red baize door, round the hall and along the passage to the white staircase. Occasionally

7 DECEMBER 1834

Lady Mary Rose, Julia and I went for our usual walk. The mud is awful and tired us a good deal. Lord Somerville and his sister, second-cousins of my mother-in-law, arrived before dinner. Lord S. has not become any wittier. His sister, on the other hand, always is.

Watercolour in a scrapbook of the cockatoo brought back from Singapore by Richard Aubrey when he was a midshipman and which stayed on in the house after its death as a ghost.

we would bicycle, but that tended to be unpopular with our elders.

The bird cage at the far end in Lili's picture seems to contain canaries. Birds, stuffed or live, appear to have been popular at the time. Richard Aubrey brought back a cockatoo from Singapore when he was a midshipman, which lived to a venerable age. It stayed on as a ghost in the house and when my mother came there in the 1930s, the house having been unoccupied for some years, she and others were convinced that they sometimes heard its disembodied voice squawking from the conservatory.

THE SOANE DRAWING ROOM   9 JANUARY 1835

DURING THE WEEK THIS WAS PAINTED, LILI HAD BEEN TO visit Lady Jersey at Middleton a few miles away; she became quite a favourite with her. This was something of an honour for Lili, since Lady Jersey was one of the leading political hostesses of the day, although Lili was close to the Bavarian Court and was acquainted with or related to many of the European aristocracy whom the Jerseys also knew. Her understanding of the international scene was far above that of the worthy but bucolic local ladies and would have had an instant appeal. Lady Jersey, who had inherited Osterley Park, entertained at both houses with style and magnificence. In her youth she had a fine singing voice which, according to the diarist Creevey, she used to display at the slightest opportunity. She also introduced into England that shocking new dance, the Waltz. I wonder if she exercised her voice at Aynhoe.

Also during this week, the house was full of guests for a local ball. The other guests would have assembled in the drawing room in excited anticipation; not Lili, however, for she found English balls dismal affairs, and in her diary recorded her relief that she had managed to avoid going to this one.

9 FEBRUARY 1835

Today I have been to Middleton to visit Lady Jersey, where I spent an hour most agreeably. She has been perfectly charming to me. Mr. and Miss Ross and Ch. Knightley have come to Aynhoe for the Banbury Ball which takes place tomorrow.

5 JANUARY 1835

Mrs. Cart. took to the Ball this evening the 2 girls, 2 Misses Holbech . . . Miss Wall, 3 young Holbech boys and Mr. Grenville Pigott. I have never been happier when they all went off to the Ball without me.

THE SOANE DRAWING ROOM, 9 JANUARY 1835

Her paintings continued with the Soane drawing room, in the centre of the house and facing to the south. The windows rise from floor to ceiling and can open high enough to give access to the long terrace and the view over what was then the deer park, with its great avenue of elm trees. Sadly these have now gone, to be replaced by a corn prairie. After the rebuild in the 1660s, the central window was the main entrance to the house.

This is the third in the sequence of rooms running the whole length of the main house, from east to west. Through the open doorway can be seen the salon, with its pink curtains, and the conservatory at the far end. Tradition had it that it was possible, when the doors were closed, to see through all the keyholes from the conservatory to the library. However, we never tried it. This room was redesigned by Soane and has rounded ends and a slightly vaulted ceiling. The curved corners were made possible by blocking up two windows. It was designed to be, and was generally used as, a music room because of the excellent acoustics imparted by its shape, although the two drawing rooms were used together whenever there were visitors.

Lili's diary does not enlighten us as to who in the family played the harp which stands by the forte piano or which members of the family sat on the twin chairs to play duets. A violin stands in the corner. Cornwallis played the 'cello, which was known as the Aynhoe Grumble. There is a delightful self portrait of him in one of the scrapbooks playing it, his thick lenses balanced on his nose. However he was in India by this time, having decided on a career in the Indian Civil Service. One of the delights of my own childhood was listening to my mother and brother playing two piano duets in this room, or joining in to sing extracts from *Oklahoma!* and other light music. On his own, my brother composed jazz and played it very competently in the style of Winifred Attwell. Lili herself was not particularly musical, although she enjoyed listening to music. In her introduction to her diary, describing her early childhood in Bavaria, she wrote: 'My aunt, who performed quite well on the harpsichord, decided to teach us to play this instrument. I infuriated this good aunt by my lack of concentration. I was punished nearly every day until I knew all of Wankel and Diabelli's sonatas by heart.'

In Lili's painting the brown fitted carpet clashes with the warm red of the comfortable sofas and even more with the purple tablecloth with its

Self-portrait pencil sketch of Cornwallis Cartwright playing his cello, which was known as the 'Aynhoe Grumble'. It seems to have been a source of some amusement in the family.

bullion fringe. This room was used by the ladies in the evening, when they would get out their embroidery or other work. There are three sewing boxes about the room and an embroidery frame on the table. The curtains are amazing, with pelmets running the whole length of the room and quantities of gold fringe. When they were drawn it must have helped to keep the room warm, although they would have pulled rather awkwardly across the bookcases. My parents did not attempt to put curtains here. It was difficult to obtain materials after the war and the yardage required made it nearly impossible.

The strangest piece of furniture in the room is the object on the right, presumably the divan. It is covered in tapestry work and it would have been used for the musicians of the family. Their footstools are nearby. The only piece of furniture which I recognize is the little octagonal table with a workbox on it which we use as a bedside table, and very unstable it is. The two end bronzes on the mantelpiece are from a set of twelve by Zoffoli intended for the library but not used there in William Ralph's time. They were probably acquired as a result of his Grand Tour, which had included a visit to St Petersburg and the Court of Catherine the Great as well as Italy. Over the fireplace hangs the portrait of a Spanish gentlemen by Van Dyck and next to it is a profile picture of an old man by the same artist. The little picture below is on slate and was painted by Alessandro Turchi. The other pictures are not identifiable.

THE DINING ROOM   23 JANUARY 1835

THE BAVARIAN WINTERS WITH WHICH LILI WAS FAMILIAR were harsher but more fun than the English ones. The Court and members of society went for sleigh rides to visit favoured inns, and torches were carried by outriders on the carriage drives to receptions and balls. Other than going for walks and contending with the mud in long skirts and light footwear, Aynhoe and the

THE DINING ROOM, 23 JANUARY 1835

English countryside provided few outdoor activities for women in winter before emancipation and the wellington boot. At this period it was not considered respectable for ladies to participate in foxhunting. Shooting in all weathers was an occupation pursued solely by the men of the family and was also a social necessity, to be offered to William Ralph's political friends who had just ensured his triumphant re-election.

Snow had arrived, to Lili's delight since it reminded her of Germany, and to the dismay of those members of the family whose sport was curtailed. She settled down to paint the dining room.

When Sir John Soane remodelled it, the end section of this room had been made into a servery by the use of pillars. The mahogany semi-circular tables in the niches on either side of these are built-in, as are the bookcases by the doors. A covered chamber pot would be kept on one of these tables for the use of the gentlemen after dinner when the ladies had left. If the ladies stayed too long and did not leave for the drawing room, a toast would be given by William Ralph to 'Lady Sitwell', a hint which generally caused them to leave. It was here that William Ralph dined with his parliamentary allies. The dining room table could seat twenty-four when fully extended; it did so when we used it at the dinner before my coming-out dance in 1957. But when Lili painted the room the table had shrunk back, its leaves removed, to seat five people, a very small number for this household.

The silver that is shown must have been in use for regular family meals of this sort. The delightful silver boxes and the entrée dish covers have wolf's head handles based on the family crest. The remainder of the silver, used only for the grander occasions, was kept in the concealed strongroom in the library. The rest was in the butler's pantry, where the butler, Gilham, and his footman must have been kept busy, polishing it with rouge powder and soft brushes. After Willy's son, Sir Fairfax, died in 1928 most of the silver was sold to help pay death duties. Prior to that it had been taken out once a year and spread out to be checked in the dining room, where it covered half the floor.

The splendid damask tablecloth was one of many that were kept in the cupboards in the housekeeper's room. After the war, when the house first opened to the public, my parents had a number of them dyed and made into curtains for several rooms, since materials were difficult to obtain and very expensive. They lasted for many years and we still have a

10 JANUARY 1835

The election of Mr. Cart. has passed off in the most triumphant manner; not only in Northampton but in all the towns he passed through on his return, where his horses were taken out, where his carriage was pulled by the people, and he arrived here at eleven in the evening, surrounded by an enormous crowd. They all arrived with laurel in their hats and shouted with endless cheers all their happiness. If all the elections were as favourable as these which are being fêted in Northamptonshire, Sir R. Peel and his ministry would be very strong.

few of the original cloths left. However, they managed to buy enough material for the dining room windows, and this was laid out on the dining table to be cut and made up by the butler's wife, Mrs Mimms. William Ralph had no such problem when the house was done up for him by 1802. Every room had lavish velvet curtains. As these survived, along with some of the upholstery and carpets, until Willy's death in 1917, it could be said that they were a good investment.

Lili shows the table set for lunch and there is a choice of red and white wine in the decanters and some remaining in the glasses. Lili had a poor head for wine and would have drunk as little as possible. The men of the family also drank beer; it was brewed in the brewhouse close to the west wing for the servants and with a special brew set aside for the family. Lili had learnt, with difficulty, to drink small quantities of beer at Sandizell, where they had a similar system. In winter, ice was obtained for the Aynhoe household from the canal, kept in the icehouse near the church and brought out when required.

The set of twelve elegant Regency chairs has long since disappeared and the table was sold when we left Aynhoe in 1960. This is the only one of the main rooms which does not have a fitted carpet but instead has one which has been woven in one piece. The two bronzes on the mantelpiece are part of the library set. The fire grate is full of coal, ready to be lit, but the large basket beyond the fireplace contains logs, so both must have been used. The three big pictures are all now in museums. The painting of the Arch of Constantine is by Gaspar Dughet, known as Poussin, and Jean Miel. It now hangs in the Fitzwilliam Museum in Cambridge. Its companion, a classical landscape probably by the same artists, is in the Barber Institute in Birmingham. The central painting is by Rembrandt and is of a boy leaning through the window of a butcher's shop and looking at two dead peacocks, a subject which suggests some strange dinner party menus among the smart set in Amsterdam. It was sold in the 1920s to the Rijksmuseum. It was not one of the artist's better efforts.

When I was growing up, we used the dining room only on special occasions, since the table was permanently laid with a service and the public were going round every day. During the war, it was the Officers' Mess. I remember it when the Army were still occupying the house and we went in there to join the officers in listening to the Derby. It was won by Dante, on which our Nanny had placed a modest sum.

THE VESTIBULE   27 JANUARY 1835

25 AND 26 JANUARY 1835

There was nothing of note today. Sunday passed like all Sundays in writing letters in the morning and in being bored in the evening . . .

We have all been to North Aston to make a visit to Lady Clonmel. The weather was magnificent and we met Lady C. who was also taking a carriage drive. I had one of my bad head colds which torment me horribly.

DESPITE WHAT MUST HAVE BEEN HER SWIMMING HEAD AND constant nose-blowing, Lili drew the vestibule with all her interested capacity for detail.

It is shown looking towards the closed library doors and the door out on to the terrace. Behind this was a small space which was probably used to keep flower trugs and dog towels, conveniently placed for the return from the garden. At the time there were several dogs in the house, their portraits lovingly painted in the scrapbooks. Julia had a small black and white animal of a hairy variety which appears in many of her paintings and, when Julia was absent, in some of Lili's. As children we had a dog which was a cross between a corgi and a dachsund. It was an inveterate hunter of rabbits in the park and had a tendency to roll in unspeakable messes. When we could stand it no longer, it would be washed in an old hip bath in a garret at the top of Soane's arch above the housekeeper's room. These problems encouraged me to favour cats.

Lili has been sitting in the doorway of the dining room, no doubt getting in the way of the staff who would be coming in and out from the door to the service wing to the left of the stairs. She shows the bottom of the cantilevered stone staircase, which is surmounted by the glazed dome. The vestibule has a curved ceiling and Lili's version of perspective makes the room look much larger than it really is. Directly below the hanging lamp at the centre of the curve there is a strong echo, which could be disconcerting for any guide standing under it when taking a party of visitors round. Many of the fine hanging lamps around the house have gone. As they were a matching set, it seems that they were part of Soane's design. The floor is tiled in the painting, but by my parents' time the tiles had been replaced by polished boards.

Two top hats stand upside down on the forte piano, one black and one grey. There is a book with a white leather binding on the shelf

20 JANUARY 1835

It has been very cold, which caused everyone to complain, except myself – I am very glad to see a bit of winter at last. Marianne, William, their two sons, Sir Robert Gunning, Ch. Litchfield and Mr. Knightley came to dine and spent the night here. I had good news from Mama of my sisters and my husband but, alas, he does not write a word about his arrival.

THE VESTIBULE, 27 JANUARY 1835

A hunting party at
Aynhoe, 1839.

below, close to the exotically embroidered stool, which probably contained music. One of Julia's paintings shows the piano open and ready for
use, which suggests that either she, or her daughter Julia, was the pianist.
The room was obviously much used, having coconut matting rugs at the
door to the library and at the bottom of the stairs, which would deter the
passage of mud into the other areas of the house. A maid with a mop
could always clean the tiles.

The collection of stuffed birds is typical of the time, although the
family were less keen on such trophies than many. (The birds ended up,
slightly moth-eaten, in our playroom.) Neither did they go in for the
sporting paintings which were becoming popular, even though they were
so keen on hunting and shooting. A pack of harriers had existed at
Aynhoe throughout the eighteenth century, originally belonging to the
first Thomas Cartwright, and had survived until Lili's time, ineffectually
piloted by young Henry and Richard Aubrey. However, they were
dispersed once regular foxhunting was available with the pack which
eventually became the Bicester. More than a hundred years later I used
to go out with them on my pony, getting to know the countryside
intimately by falling off in it. This was a minor embarrassment to my
father, who had earlier banned the hunt from the park after they had
galloped over his new grass tennis courts.

To the right of the library door is a cabinet with an assortment of
objects on display. At the top hangs something that looks like a horsetail
plume, perhaps from the days of William Ralph's uncle who had been a
general, or even a relic from Waterloo where Lili's brother-in-law,
William, had fought. His letters from that campaign still exist, along
with his diary. Below this are porcelain figurines and some archaeological
items. These appear to include an Egyptian necklace and two Roman

bottles which may have been acquired by Richard Aubrey on his travels as a midshipman.

We still have the pair of Georgian mahogany stools with their cane seats. The bookcase or cabinet has a metal grille but became an open china cabinet later. The curtains, with their complicated pelmets, pull only from one side, like those in the Soane drawing room, and are held back by brass roundels. They are of velvet, like most of the other curtains in the house. Of the pictures, I can only recognize the one between the windows, a studio copy of a Beechey of George III on horseback, and the one over the case of humming birds, a portrait by Ferdinand Bol.

THE LIBRARY   5 FEBRUARY 1835

The Cartwright family's book plate.

LILI SEEMS TO HAVE BEEN A LITTLE CASUAL ABOUT HER SMALL son Tommy, now four years old, who had recently arrived from Munich, and about whom she makes little comment. When everyone had left after the baptism she could get back to her picture of the library in peace and quiet, Tommy having been consigned, no doubt, to the nursery out of earshot.

The library is the last of the long suite of rooms running the entire length of the house on the side facing the park. This block, which includes the vestibule, was added by Archer in 1707 to the post-Civil War house to match the conservatory at the other end, but the interior is by Soane. The cornices are arched above the bookshelves, where the set of bronzes was intended to stand. The big windows at the far end look out over the garden to the west where there is, and always was, a small formal garden with geometric flowerbeds centred on a sundial. These sash windows open on to it from ground level for easy access to this area, provided that the members of this tall family remembered to duck low enough. Lili, of course, had no such problem.

To start her painting she sat down with her back to one of the folio cases, with the double doors of the library behind her to the left. The

4 FEBRUARY 1835

Tommy was baptized in the church today at midday. Robert, who is one of the godparents, came to assist at the ceremony. The church was very crowded. Tommy conducted himself very well. The weather was quite magnificent.

THE LIBRARY, 5 FEBRUARY 1835

bookcases on the left hide the exit from the vestibule to the terrace on the south front. At the far side of the window recess is the strongroom, concealed behind the bookshelves, where generations of butlers kept the silver that was not regularly in use, along with family documents, jewellery and assorted valuables. Security was, perhaps, less of a problem in her day than in this century. Apart from the awesome penalties of being caught, any burglar might have been deterred by the task of breaking down locked wooden shutters with spring bells attached to them without disturbing some of the twenty-two servants, numerous family, several dogs and the cockatoo. There were anxieties at the time about public disorders, rather than private security, since there were riots going on in many parts of the country because of the price of corn and the introduction of machines to replace traditional skills. A few weeks previously, Lili had watched the distant glow of fires from burning rickyards a few miles away.

The library is shown with a fitted carpet. This was probably woven specially at Axminster or Wilton along with those in the other rooms. Once again, the curtains are hung asymmetrically. The furniture is mostly Regency, as a great deal of furniture would have been purchased when the house was refurbished to match the new style, but there are a few items from the previous century, such as the pair of Chinese Chippendale chairs and two armchairs. We still have the small Georgian tables, the armchairs with curved backs, the sofa tables at the far end and the splendid terrestrial and sidereal globes.

There were about four thousand books in the library, the majority still in the family though no longer at Aynhoe. Richard Cartwright's original library was burned by the Royalist troops, but Thomas Cartwright restocked the collection. Many volumes have his bookplate in them and his comments in the margin. He acquired a large quantity of religious works of paralysing obscurity, books on travel (which perhaps he wanted to do but never did), history, philosophy, science and politics. On the table by the fireplace Lili shows a brown book which I believe to be a volume of political cartoons, their colours vulgar and their sentiments violently anti-Catholic. On the big table by the window lie several books, one of which may be a delightful French manuscript of the *Lives of the Philosophers* and another a volume of drawings by Palma Giovane.

24 FEBRUARY 1835

The Ministers keep up appearances: they do not have an anxious air; they continue to debate and are being battered by the Opposition until they swear to vote for Church Reform which is a measure which can only please the opposing faction. If it is from love of mischief, they will regret it as Parliament will be suspended which terrifies everyone and the country will be thrown back into the greatest agitation from which there will be a very different outcome.

The library was my favourite room as a child, with its smells of dusty leather, polish and old rugs. On rainy days I would spend happy hours sitting on the oak floorboards (the fitted carpet long since departed), taking out folios from the lower shelves. Naturally I preferred the ones with illustrations at first. There was Sir William Hamilton's set depicting his collection of Greek and Etruscan pottery and his work on the Campi Phlegrae, with landscapes and the excavations at Pompeii in gorgeous colour, unfaded by the sun. The volumes of natural history were the best, such as the *History of Four-Footed Beasts and Serpents* by Topsell and Mufet, 1658, or Albin on *British Insects*. Then there was the Duke of Newcastle on *Horses*, with engravings of himself showing off on various steeds with large behinds, surrounded by admirers. There were flower books, such as *Flora Monacencis* and *The Botanical Magazine*. Best of all, there was *The Gentleman's Recreation* by Blome, 1686, which had detailed instructions on such diverse things as how to catch eels, prune apple trees, build a classical mansion, learn mathematics or conduct a war. I do not know if my parents realized that their eleven-year-old daughter was regularly thumbing through some very rare volumes, but they never tried to stop me.

In the nineteenth century the library was considered the men's preserve, although all the family used it from time to time. Here William Ralph would discuss politics with his friends, and catch up on the newspapers which had been delivered by coach or on his letters, which had come with the postboy. It was also the place for family rows. No doubt, after his recent election success, he retired here for a celebratory glass of port which would not have improved his gout.

My parents used the library for drinks before dinner if there were guests and for occasional parties. When the guides were taking people round the house in the 1950s, on several occasions when they had just left the room with their parties, they would hear men's voices talking in the library and would go back to collect the non-existent people they thought they had left behind. It could, of course, have had something to do with the echo in the vestibule, but it caused some perplexity.

MRS CARTWRIGHT'S SITTING ROOM   25 FEBRUARY 1835

THE WEATHER WAS ATROCIOUS, AND VISITORS FEW, WHICH gave Lili leisure to paint her mother-in-law's sitting room in minute detail.

Directly above the library and overlooking the little formal garden, this room has a domed ceiling and curved cornices. The matching curtains and upholstery, of printed material with sprigs of flowers, is feminine and charming. Once again, the fitted carpet looks as if it was woven for the room. The furniture is mostly light and pretty, even allowing for Lili's style of drawing which tends to elongate it. With her Bavarian background, it is as if she saw furniture with eyes tuned to expect the Biedermeier pieces with which she was more familiar. There is only one fully upholstered chair, but there are four chaises-longues, which suggests that Julia was able to put her feet up out of the draughts when not working at her baize-covered sofa table by the window. Considering how busy she was, it seems unlikely that she would have had much time to do so, though Lili's diary suggests that the family sometimes sat here during the evenings.

On a table is a letter and an inkstand with a quill pen in it. The chair is set askew, as if she had recently left her work. On the table with the red cover are watercolours of birds and flowers, perhaps to be placed in her scrapbook later or given to members of the family. Julia also wrote poetry competently, some of which appears in her scrapbook, and read widely. The bookcases, though, have blue curtains in front of them, to protect the bindings from fading but making it look as if it was thought indelicate for a lady to have too great an interest in books.

There is a total absence of lamps, in this room as in all others. The oil lamps would be brought in by the servants every evening as required throughout the occupied portions of the house. Many of our own lamps are the same ones, converted, with varying degrees of success, to

25 FEBRUARY 1835

The weather was really wild today, and since there was no chance of going out, I drew all day.

Mrs Cartwright's Sitting Room, 25 February 1835

electricity. Julia seems to have had a taste for knick-knacks, which must have caused problems for the housemaid, as they stand insecurely along the row of tables and bookcases. Among the group of paintings on the wall above them are two small pictures by Murillo of Christ and the Madonna. Round them are a set of small seascapes on copper by Swaine and two Italian paintings on black slate, one of them by Albani. The pictures at the far end of the room are not identifiable, but around the fireplace are a group of drawings of members of the family by Edridge. The charming little drawing of a mother and child is of Julia herself with her son Henry. These are still in the family.

When we lived at Aynhoe, this sitting room was my father's dressing room, dark and gloomy and full of unlikely objects which had been dumped there for some reason and had never been evicted, such as several carpets, some sets of plaster casts of classical intaglios, numerous pairs of beautifully polished shoes in a line, a first edition of Fraser's *Golden Bough*, a meteorite and a patent Turkish bath. Although I recall the room then as being rather forbidding, when Julia occupied it it appears light and cheerful, with its charming little alcove looking out over the park.

3 FEBRUARY 1835

I had many letters from Munich where they speak of many feasts and balls and Mama has, by the Grace of God, completely recovered. Caroline [one of Lili's sisters] can join the pleasures of Carnival. Mr. and Mrs. Carter, Miss Murray and Miss Kent, as well as Marianne and Frank, arrived today.

Julia's painting of her own sitting room from her album of interiors. The women of the family would use this room on informal occasions, although it was intended as the place to which Julia could escape from family and guests.

MR CARTWRIGHT'S STUDY   2 MARCH 1835

L ILI WAS WAITING ANXIOUSLY FOR NEWS OF HER HUSBAND'S
arrival in England after her stay of some six months so far.
William Ralph had been suffering from a severe attack of gout
for several weeks. He had a relapse after attempting to go back
to work too soon, stimulated by the unstable condition of the Tory
administration which had recently ousted the Whigs, and had gone back
to bed. It is clear from the state of the room (and the fact that Lili had an
opportunity to paint it at all) that he was not able to spend much time
here. Everything is regimentally tidy, a state that would have been
unlikely under normal working conditions. The fire in the steel grate is
not laid.

The study lies between the hall and the stone staircase (which Lili
started to draw but did not finish) and it faces north towards the
courtyard and the village. Because of its position it gets little sun, and it
seems that the bright sunlight and shadow bars on the shutters could only
have existed around noon. The bottoms of the windows are shaded to
stop people looking in. It is a comfortable working room, small and fully
carpeted, with one upholstered chair which is similar to the one in the
music room. There is a lockable document box in blue leather on the
desk, along with an inkstand and penholder with a carrying handle,
several books, a letter and some writing paper. The roll-top desk is closed
and on top of it is a holder for writing paper and a set of delicate letter
scales. Beyond it is a sofa table which we still use and there are more
books on it, possibly the latest editions of the *Parliamentary Register*. The
contents of the bookcases look as if they are mainly works of reference
and on the top shelves there appear to be boxes for documents, bills or
letters. There is a barometer by the window, which must have been
useful for predicting the weather for the long journey by post chaise to
the Sessions in Northampton where William Ralph was a magistrate. His
hats, one black and one grey, hang on the peg alongside his umbrella.

24 FEBRUARY 1835

*Sir Henry Peyton, and Mr.
Carter [of Edgecott] came to
visit Mr. Cart. who got up today
for the first time but who is far
from being over his attack of
gout and his fever. The political
news from London is bad. Sir
Robert Peel is expecting a
majority of 41 against him when
voting takes place over the
address to the King.*

Mr Cartwright's Study, 2 March 1835

The religious picture over the fireplace is a rather indifferent scene by a follower of Murillo of an angel soliciting a startled monk. We sold it. The portraits on the wall are, from left to right: Ferdinando, Lord Fairfax, a competent cavalry commander during the Civil War. His youngest daughter, conceived when he was in his eighties, married the first William Cartwright; next, his father, the first Baron Cameron, who seems to have thought little of him despite his military achievements, and finally General Sir Thomas Fairfax, Ferdinando's son, who was the Commander-in-Chief of the Parliamentarian forces, creator of the New Model Army and thus Cromwell's military superior.

Above the door hangs a map, rolled up, and there are two more over the bookcases. We know that one of these was a map of the county and the other an estate map from Julia's painting of the same room. The estate map would have been more up to date than the one made in 1697, just before the first enclosures of the communal village fields took place during Thomas Cartwright's tenure, with an acrimony typical of Aynho affairs but with reasonable fairness in the end. That map is currently in the Northamptonshire County Record Office along with the rest of the family documents and letters. The final enclosures were made during William Ralph's minority.

We used this room as our dining room since it was relatively small, comfortable and, above all, warm. Its earliest known name was 'The Justices' Room', perhaps from the period of Thomas Cartwright, when it must have served some function of the magistracy or, more probably, the Manor Court. The little room next door, originally known as 'The Prisoners' Room' was our butler's pantry, and just beyond the side entrance to the house was our kitchen. My parents made these alterations because the original kitchen and dining room were some thirty-five yards apart.

THE SCHOOLROOM   10 MARCH 1835

17 MARCH 1835

This morning's post brought us sad news; Lizzy Gunning died in London yesterday during the aftermath of the operation which was performed on her eight days ago. This news has saddened us all greatly. What increased my unhappiness was a letter which I had from Cart. which has destroyed all hope of seeing him in England.

24 MARCH 1835

Mary and Henry Gunning arrived today and we were very happy to see them so calm and resigned. They will stay here until the end of next week. They brought me the portraits of Cart. and of my dear Willy which I find little like them. Mr. Cart. has left his room and come down and even dined with us. which must give him much pleasure after his imprisonment of six weeks.

LILI'S DIARY DURING THIS MONTH SERVES AS A REMINDER OF THE precariousness of life and of the difficulty of communication over any distance in the early part of the nineteenth century. Lizzy Gunning's brother, Henry, had married Mary Cartwright, and they were all frequent visitors to Aynhoe. Another brother had also met an early death: a friend of William Cartwright, who fought with him throughout the Peninsular War, he was killed at Waterloo.

Lili was now beginning to despair of seeing her husband and Willy again in the near future, and was not much consoled when their portraits, commissioned by Sir Thomas, arrived. No doubt she wished that Willy could have been making use of the schoolroom which she now settled down to paint.

Her youngest sisters-in-law, Fanny and Julia, were still using the schoolroom. Having had thirteen children occupying it in turn over the previous thirty years or so, it had been very well used; the magnificent fitted carpet seems to have survived in remarkably good condition although the wallpaper looks a little tired. I think this room must be on the top floor, probably facing north, but I cannot place it. The bottoms of the windows are shaded, not to prevent people looking in, as in William Ralph's study, but to stop the children looking, and more importantly from falling, out. The curtains are bunched at the top of the windows and pull downwards via the blue ropes. The firescreens are in a matching blue material.

The schoolroom table in the centre of the room is made of a slightly unpleasant-looking red mahogany. It was the table in our playroom as it is in our son's and has acquired a delicate pattern of saw cuts round the edge thanks to my juvenile experiments in carpentry. Julia or Fanny has

Wash drawing of Lili's husband, Thomas, in 1835. This, and its companion portrait of their son Willy, was sent to Aynhoe to Lili who was disappointed with the likenesses.

THE SCHOOLROOM, 10 MARCH 1835

been painting a landscape. The paintbox is on the left and a plate to the right acts as a palette. A large wine glass for water is behind it. The table between the windows has an inkstand and some books. All the chairs look a little uncomfortable except for the well-used upholstered armchair in the corner, with its printed cover. Underneath the roll-top desk is a small cabinet for a collection of birds' eggs or geological specimens. There are a number of large books about the room and some small ones on the shelves. The wall map appears to show India. The globe must also have been a help for geography lessons, and the two wastepaper baskets useful for paper darts, botched exercises and rude messages to be concealed from the governess.

Out of place in this modest room is the big, ornate lacquered cabinet, dating from the time of Charles II, on a heavily carved stand. There were three of these in the house. A visiting furniture expert was kind enough to explain to me recently that this was a late nineteenth-century copy. I can only assume it was in the schoolroom as such pieces were out of fashion by William Ralph's time. The clock, perhaps for timing the length of lessons and making sure that the children arrived on time for meals, stands on top of it. There are two silhouettes over the picture of the horse above the fireplace. To the right hangs a copy of the Arch of Constantine which hung in the dining room. It might have been drawn by one of the family.

Fanny and Julia as adolescents, puppy fat still visible, looking at books in the library. Coloured pencil drawing from Marianne's scrapbook; about 1840.

Julia's painting of the schoolroom from her book of interiors. Influenced by Lili, she too had become a dedicated painter of interiors.

[55]

Lili Abroad

1835–45

2 MARCH 1835

Mr. Cart. who has the greatest desire to see Cart. has written to him today to ask him to come and see him. Oh, how happy I will be if he asks for leave and has it granted to him. I ask Heaven daily to be given the joy of seeing him in England and hope that God, in his Divine mercy, will grant my wishes.

THE SCHOOLROOM WAS THE LAST OF LILI'S PAINTINGS FROM her visit of 1835. She was indeed to see Thomas soon, but not in England, for he was unable to take leave. Instead, Lili rejoined him in Brussels at the beginning of May.

She was delighted to be back with her husband and elder son and to be mistress of her own house again. Soon after she rejoined him, Thomas was transferred to Frankfurt, where he received a knighthood for his work in Brussels and during the siege of Antwerp. For the next ten years she continued to lead the life of a diplomat's wife. She also continued to paint. While she was in Frankfurt she made the acquaintance of Mary Ellen Best, an English lady resident in Frankfurt who also painted interiors and portraits but did so professionally. It is possible that she may have helped Lili with her painting.

The family settled down happily in the city in a house which Lili loved and which had a good garden for the children. There were visits from various members of the Cartwright family who came out to stay with them; Henry, Aubrey and Robert were all guests, as well as their sister Mary and her husband, Henry Gunning. It was one of the happiest periods of her life, despite their perpetual worries about young Willy's health.

Her husband's duties and the increasing demands on their limited finances made it difficult for them to visit England for more than two short visits in the next ten years. Lili entertained a great deal, went to the opera, met anyone of interest who came to Frankfurt and travelled to her own home at Sandizell whenever she could. She commented knowledgeably and with acute observation on the political events of the Continent and the characters of those she met who were involved. Sir Thomas worked with dedication to carry out the many difficult negotiations with which he was entrusted.

A few years later, Sir Thomas was transferred to Sweden as British Minister, a move which distressed Lili because of the isolation from her own German family which it entailed and the loss of their much-loved house. She was homesick for Germany for some time, but eventually resigned herself to her new home. Her sons grew up, educated by tutors, speaking German more easily than English, and having, at that stage, only a dim memory of Aynhoe. However, there were other new interests to comment on in her diary. She spent much time in and around the Swedish Court of King Oscar, whom she had already met some years before when he visited Munich before his marriage, and Queen Josephina. King Oscar was the son of Napoleon's former general Bernadotte who had been offered the crown of Sweden by the Swedes, and Josephina was the grand-daughter of the Empress Josephine. One of the family scrapbooks has a charming little sketch of Willy and Tommy skiing and sledging with the royal children at Malmö, which may be one of the earliest pictures of a skiing party. This drawing had been sent by Lili to her mother-in-law, Julia, with whom she corresponded regularly.

By 1844, both Lili and Sir Thomas had developed an anxious relationship with Willy, who was nineteen. He was frequently ill and seems to have been accident-prone. His ailments and probably hypochondria surfaced whenever he was faced with a situation he did not wish to encounter. He was also highly intelligent, romantic and disinclined to do any work unless it interested him. Like his brother Tommy, he had

Ink drawing by Lili of a Swedish lady in full court mourning dress which she sent to Julia in a letter.

Watercolour sketch by Lili of Willy and Tommy skiing with the Swedish royal family, Sir Thomas having been sent to Stockholm as British Minister.

spent nearly all his boyhood abroad and seems to have had little interest in England at that time, which lent urgency to his parents wish for them all to visit Aynhoe again. They seem to have had a more relaxed relationship with Tommy, now fourteen, who had always been much easier to deal with. This pattern continued during much of their later lives, with Tommy behaving conventionally and Willy having a stormy but more interesting life and invariably upsetting his mother.

In 1844, Willy had been ill for a year and had been sent to Switzerland to recuperate. He had been unable to take up his place at Balliol College, Oxford, because of his health – not that he had the

29 AUGUST 1845

Willy and I dined at four and at five-thirty we left on the Great Western Railway for Oxford where we arrived a little before eight o'clock; from there we took post horses to go to Aynhoe where we arrived at ten in the evening. I had the pleasure of finding Tommy and all the family in good health; everyone is reunited. I find myself really happy to be here at last with my sons and after a journey which has fatigued me considerably.

slightest wish to go there, but his father was insistent that he should do so. Tommy was also destined for Oxford and had been given a tutor, Mr Algar, to prepare him for the entrance examination to the same college. His parents felt that it was essential for them to spend some time in England to see the family after such a long gap and to be with their sons while they prepared for, and settled in at, Oxford. In any case, Sir Thomas, abetted by Lili, felt that after some five years in Sweden, his career had stagnated and that it was desirable to go to London to talk to Lord Aberdeen in the hope of obtaining a higher diplomatic post. It may be that they feared, as had happened in 1835, that William Ralph's identification with the Tory party hindered his son's career during the Whig administrations, and the Whigs were now in power. They could not afford to go to England at this point, but felt that they must sacrifice everything to do so if necessary. However, Sir Thomas wrote successfully to his father for financial help to avoid putting his career at risk.

As soon as it was confirmed that Willy was to return to England and take another entrance examination for Oxford, he developed whooping cough. Leeches were applied 'to starve the illness', which made him too weak to travel. This meant that he missed his examination once again and would have to have it postponed. Lili became worried and depressed over her family problems. Some months later, in August 1845, they all arrived back at Aynhoe. To Lili's great relief, since she was deeply suspicious of horse-drawn transport from long experience, there was now a railway from London to Oxford and its extension to Banbury was soon to be built. The journey took two-and-a-half hours from Paddington, as long as a scheduled flight to Cairo these days, and then they had a two-hour carriage drive with post horses to the house.

Most of the family were regular visitors to Aynhoe still, though more deeply settled into their respective lives after the ten-year gap, and the house was busier than ever. Fanny and Julia were still at home, the only unmarried daughters, but their weddings were imminent. William Ralph, at seventy-four years old, was still an MP, but his political life had become a little less strenuous. Henry, about to rejoin his regiment, was at home. Richard Aubrey had retired from the Navy and now had the expectation of inheriting Edgecott from his mother's connections, the Carters. Cornwallis was still in India; Stephen had taken on the living at Aynhoe and was now the Rector, though apparently disliked by most of

13 SEPTEMBER 1845

Cart. left for London today in order to present himself to Lord Aberdeen who has returned. May God grant that his interview will prove favourable and that it will one day lead to advancement in his diplomatic career. Aynhoe was really depopulated today; not less than 18 people including the valets left this morning; Marianne, together with Fanny and Henry, went with Sir Thomas Aubrey to Oving, where the first meeting of Mr. Boulton with Fanny will take place. He is on his way to England and it was suggested to him that he see Fanny again at Oving (being a very shy man) before he comes to claim her at Aynhoe where he will find himself immediately in a large family party of which he will not know three-quarters.

Portrait of William as a handsome young man in his uniform of the 11th Hussars. Drawing from Julia's scrapbook by an unknown hand.

Watercolour drawing of Marianne with her dogs by Josiah Dighton. Marianne and William were frequent visitors to Aynhoe.

the family including Lili. William had married Marianne Jones, an heiress with London property, before Lili's first visit. Family legend has it that when he was with his regiment, the 10th Hussars, a few years after Waterloo, the young officers had drawn lots to decide who should pay court to Marianne first. William won the short straw and the lady. It was a happy marriage and the couple were now living at Flore House near Northampton. William was still a colonel in the Army, but on half-pay. Lili got on well with Marianne, who was fun. All the daughters except Julia and Fanny were married. As soon as Lili and her family had arrived, her husband and sons joined Henry and Aubrey in foxhunting, with great enthusiasm. It was a relief that Willy had found something English at which to be reasonably competent and to enjoy, since he was a hopelessly poor shot, to his parent's dismay.

Lili, at forty, was sophisticated, more confident of her position within the family, mildly inclined to depression and fears for the future, but as observant as ever and even more able to express her feelings, and to record in her paintings and in her diary the changes which had taken place in the house and the family since her last long stay there. Her

19 SEPTEMBER 1845

The gentlemen are going shooting regularly and daily. Willy goes with them, but whether it is because of poor eyesight or whether it is just incompetence, he never kills his partridge and if the poor birds had no other enemies but him they would multiply at their ease . . .

13 OCTOBER 1845

Today was a great day for Willy and Tommy; they went foxhunting and spent a great part of the day on horseback crossing the country; the meet took place at Astrop; from there the hunt went towards Hinton and Brackley. Five hunters from this house took part in the hunt, namely Aubrey, Henry, Willy, Tommy and George Gunning.

religion was a great comfort to her in her times of unhappiness, though it was difficult to practise it at Aynhoe.

William Ralph was thinking of retiring from politics, but Julia was still entertaining his friends and the hordes of relatives and connections of the younger generation. Fanny and Julia were about to marry and their weddings were preoccupying the family. Lili's diary is full of trenchant comments about the young man, Edward Goulbourn, whom Julia was to marry, and the unfavourable contrast between him and Matthew Boulton (grandson of the inventor) of Great Tew Park who, despite his shyness and cold manner, was Fanny's choice. (My Italian grandmother used to make exactly the same irritated comments about the English manner – so frustrating for those of a more volatile temperament.) While all this was going on, and while her husband and sons joined in the shooting parties and hunting in which the men were involved, Lili continued with her series of interiors. The style shows a marked improvement. By this time she was running out of rooms in the main house. She painted a few bedrooms and went on to the service wing, and after that she went out into the village, sometimes with her mother-in-law and sometimes alone, to paint the interiors of some of the cottages.

30 AUGUST 1845

I find Aynhoe more beautiful than ever; the garden is so well laid out; there is a mass of flowers there; the park is still so beautiful, so fresh, so green. The weather has been superb today and we have even found it too hot. We walked together a great deal, some on horses, others on foot; still others played cricket; one does not lack for amusements in England.

William Ralph Cartwright MP. Watercolour by Josiah Dighton. Although he is portrayed riding his sensible cob, William Ralph made his journeys to the Sessions in Northampton or to the House of Commons by post-chaise.

Lili's Paintings

1845–47

THE SALON   5 NOVEMBER 1845

EDWARD GOULBOURN SEEMS TO HAVE BEEN SOMETHING OF A prig. His unspecified solecisms regarding the marriage settlement were exceeded in Lili's unforgiving eyes only by those of his father. The wedding, which finally took place in December, was preceded by a considerable amount of financial wrangling and unedifying behaviour on the part of the family and of gloomy foreboding on the part of Lili. (Some years later Edward Goulbourn became the headmaster of Rugby School. School entries dropped alarmingly over a period, but the trustees were unable to remove him until, to their relief, he was elevated to the position of Dean of Norwich.) As the wedding approached, Lili's reflections grew correspondingly more lugubrious. Mr Goulbourn was no doubt received very coldly more than once in the drawing room which she had begun to paint.

Lili's skill in painting had improved immeasurably in the ten years since her last interiors of the Aynhoe rooms. One of her first attempts then was of the salon and she must have been dissatisfied with it, judging by the trouble she took over the second one. Several things had changed. The chairs and the sofas had been re-covered, the Regency striped velvet having gone out of fashion, with a material with a pattern of small flowers. The splendidly draped curtains and the carpet with its trellis pattern remain unchanged, perhaps because they were the most expensive items to alter. The tablecloths also have flower patterns with heavy blue velvet edging and long fringes. The new upholstery goes with the walls which have been painted a soft gold colour, making the room lighter and more friendly than in previous years when it was painted grey.

27 OCTOBER 1845

Mr. Goulbourn arrived today and was received very coldly, as he deserved. He had a conference with Julia at the end of which he renounced his allowance and will be content to live at Oxford on £700, little enough it is true, but if Julia agrees to an arrangement of that sort, it seems that he has no right to complain.

8 NOVEMBER 1845

During the four days that Mrs. Cart. and Julia spent in London, Mr. Goulbourn, senior, never went to see them once; he really ought to see Mrs. Cart. but it is unpardonable not to go and see his future daughter-in-law. This man, with his violent humour, his rapacity and many other bad qualities will be the greatest burden in Julia's future life. As to the son, he has progressed no further in the affection of his future brothers and sisters-in-law. He too has imperfections which inspire no confidence for the future happiness of this excellent and angelic Julia.

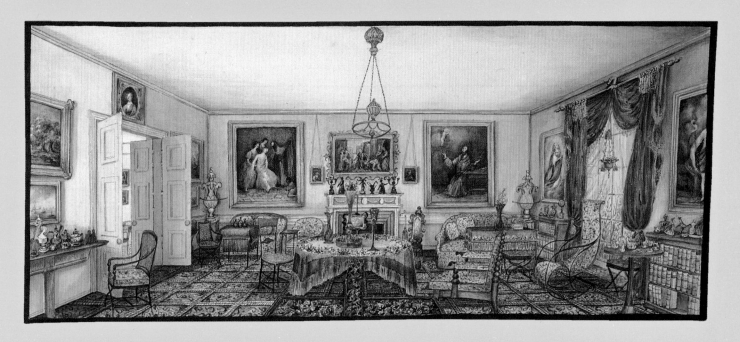

THE SALON, 5 NOVEMBER 1845

However, there are no pieces of embroidery, unfinished paintings or scrapbooks around as in her earlier picture and in Julia's paintings of the same room, which suggests that it was no longer in regular use by the family in the evenings.

Lili has been sitting by the tall windows, which face south. Through the open double doors we can catch a glimpse of the music room and to the right, through the glass doors, can be seen the conservatory. These doors look as if they were not used, as the rocking chair stands in front of them and the revolting green glass lamp with its red tassels hangs quite low from behind the curtain rail. Numerous plants in flower can be seen in the conservatory. This was one of the few main rooms which was not much altered by Soane.

The pictures hang in the same positions as they had for the past forty years, which is not surprising in view of the size of some of them and the difficulty of finding adequate wall space for the bigger pictures, even in a house the size of Aynhoe. Over the double doors hangs a portrait of Mary Desaguliers by Hogarth, always one of my favourites because of her vivacity and humour, so well portrayed by the artist. She was the grand-daughter of the great seaman of the extraordinary name, Sir Cloudesley Shovel, and daughter of John Blackwood, the art dealer and collector. She is portrayed as a girl in the splendid painting by Alan Ramsay of Lord Mansell and his half-brothers and sister which was recently purchased by the Tate Gallery. She left many of her father's paintings to her grandson, William Ralph Cartwright, including the seven by Murillo shown in this room. The first, to the right of the fireplace, is of the *Vision of St Anthony* and it now hangs in the Barber Institute in Birmingham. Next to it, in the corner, is the *Assumption of the Virgin*, which is in the Museum at Fort Worth, Texas. The third is of St John with the Lamb, and his arm and one leg can be seen to the right of the picture. The two landscapes to the left, *Abraham and Isaac* and *Tobias and the Angel*, are partially hidden, and are also by Murillo, as are the two small pictures of Christ and the Madonna on either side of the fireplace. Over it hangs a Nativity scene by an unknown Italian artist.

The tops of the bookcases and the side tables are covered in small objects of porcelain and glass. We have seen Julia's penchant for knick-knacks in her sitting room and it seems to have surfaced again here, perhaps for the very good reason that the numerous members of the family were always giving her things which she felt obliged to display. There are several porcelain figurines, jugs and teapots and on a stand a large watch the size of a grapefruit. The large vases and covers in the corners of the room, protected by ropes from the more vigorous assaults of the housemaids, remain from the earlier period. On the other hand, the taste for rather nasty coloured Venetian glass vases is consistent, and must have been Julia's own.

The interest in collecting seems to have come into the family at this time, through Julia and through Lili herself. She had already started to acquire glass and porcelain in Munich, and she records in her diary many of her expeditions to auctions and dealers. She was given several porcelain groups by the Queen of Bavaria who had them specially made as gifts to court favourites. Those given to Lili were left by her to Tommy and ended up at Rousham Park in Oxfordshire. Willy collected Chinese porcelain, books, late Italian paintings and superb glass. His son, Fairfax, collected French furniture, Persian rugs and pottery and some Chinese porcelain. My father sold the previous collections of Chinese porcelain, which were less than excellent, and created a unique one of his own which was entirely of monochromes. He built a special room close to the conservatory to house them a few years after the war, made of whatever bits and pieces of materials were available. They looked magnificent even if the cabinets were made out of hardboard. Much of the glass collection occupied two cabinets in the drawing room, roughly where Lili had been sitting. Owing to the eccentricities of the wiring system, there were many occasions when the lighting in them would start to smoulder and they would have to be turned off before the public were allowed in.

Wash drawing by Lili of the exterior of Aynhoe church where the weddings of Fanny and young Julia had taken place and where her own sons had been christened.

22 DECEMBER 1845

E.G. left this evening for Oxford. If only he had never set foot at Aynhoe! We went to Brackley to see a pig which Marianne has been fattening and which is truly the most monstrous beast I have ever seen.

THE PINK BEDROOM   9 FEBRUARY 1846

27 NOVEMBER 1845

*The ceremony took place today
at eleven o'clock, in the church
... Fanny and her husband left
immediately for London and
tomorrow they will go to Dover.
The lunch was served at half
past one; the favours of all
kinds, the wedding cakes, the
sound of the bells, the post
horses decorated with white
cockades, all this has been most
scrupulously observed, and the
solemnization passed as
brilliantly as could be. The
weather was fine and the sun
was shining while we were in
church. This day has been
exhausting and we all went to
bed with headaches.*

WITH ALL THE COMINGS AND GOINGS IN THE HOUSE, Lili's bedroom must have been a haven where she could mull over her anxieties about her family and escape from the intense emotions aroused by the rest of the Cartwright family's affairs, fascinated though she was by them. She noted every detail of Fanny's wedding with delighted approval. By modern standards the celebrations she describes at Great Tew seem extremely lavish. No wonder the entire party retired to bed with headaches. At the same time she was busy recording in great detail the drama of her father-in-law's resignation as MP. He had been intending this for some time, but had taken this opportunity to implement it in order to emphasize his opposition to the reform of the Corn Laws recently brought in by his party.

Lili painted only three of the bedrooms, the pink bedroom and those of her two sons, although there are several pictures of other bedrooms by Julia. It was the main guest room at the time and it seems likely that this is the one in which she and her husband were staying, although it is not mentioned in her diary and it looks exceptionally tidy. It would have been easier to paint her own room than any of the others since there was such a constant flow of visitors. It is situated on the first floor in the centre of the main block, facing north and directly over the hall. It is a big room, although Lili makes it look small, and it has the apsidal end so typical of Soane. Behind the bed where Lili has been sitting there is a flat partition wall. Originally this room and its neighbour, a little bedroom with a similar curved end, were one even larger room. This suggests that there was a need for more guest rooms even in that enormous house.

The cupboard doors are beautifully made on the curve, and the space between the curved plaster wall and the structural walls has been turned

28 NOVEMBER 1845

*... all our gentlemen went to
Great Tew, where they had an
excellent shoot; they found Tew
celebrating and joyful, for Mr.
Boulton made celebrations for
his marriage there by giving a
feast for 400 people, and three
public balls took place the same
evening which lasted until four
o'clock in the morning, and the
rest are still going on. There
was also a feast at Aynhoe,
where an ox was roasted. I
spent the day with a headache
following the emotions and
fatigues consequent on such
events.*

THE PINK BEDROOM, 9 FEBRUARY 1846

3 FEBRUARY 1846

Mr. Cart. has inserted notice of his resignation in the papers, and of his acceptance of the Chiltern Hundreds, a form used by those who resign their seats during the existing parliament; there have been many resignations of this kind. the measures of Sir R[obert] P[eel] upset many MPs as they are not in accordance with the principles which these gentlemen have professed up till now, and even less with those of the individuals who have voted for them during their elections. They act honourably in this, it seems to me, in withdrawing themselves from a field where they are obliged to vote against their conscience or according to their opinion in favour of Sir R.P. at the risk of offending their constituents, or to abandon him in order to please the latter. Sir R.P. with his mind and eminent talent always inspires them with some confidence; Mr. Cart. has moreover his age and his health which are against the continual fatigues which will be caused in the Chamber by the debates which are about to begin.

to practical use. Perhaps because of this there is no wardrobe to be seen. When I knew the house there were a number of Georgian and Victorian wardrobes about, of suitably large proportions. The one in my bedroom, looking quite modest in size against a large wall, smelt of raw mahogany, mothballs and the delicious contents of 'care' parcels which were sent to us for several years after the war from our American foster family, the Moseleys of New Jersey.

The decorative plaster of the cornice has been painted pink to match the curtains, and strips of matching wallpaper have been used to emphasize the doors, the dado line and the end of the curved wall. The bell-pull ends in a magnificent pink tassel. The pattern of the wallpaper is difficult to see and it looks as if there is a damp patch high up on the wall by the curtains; if so, it would be entirely in keeping with the habits of the house as I knew it.

Once again, the curtains draw from one side only. The upholstered dressing table matches their colour. Like the covers of the ottoman, the armchair and the sofa, it looks as if it had retained its now unfashionable stripes from forty years earlier. The carpet is fitted and there are two rugs. The chequered one appears as if it might have been home-made. There are glass cosmetic boxes on the dressing table, looking under-employed, and a set of china toilet ware is on the wash stand. The fireplace has a fire lit and in front of it, cosily positioned in such a large, cold room, is a table

Watercolour by Julia of the bedroom shared by her two daughters. Fanny and Julia used the room until they were married within a few weeks of each other.

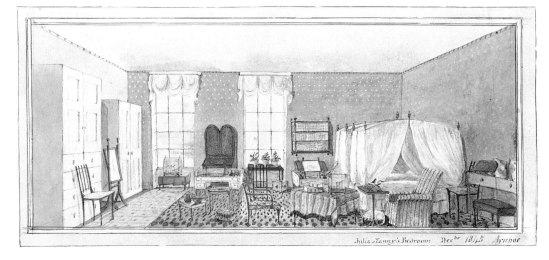

Julia & Fanny's Bedroom Dec.r 1845 Aynhoe

5 FEBRUARY 1846

The post brought a number of letters to Mr. Cartwright, all relating to his resignation. He is greatly relieved to have finished this affair. Many other resignations have taken place ... The farmers are in accord in not leaving their seats quietly in this parliament which has voted in favour of Free Trade. Mr. Cartwright laid down his position, making it quite clear that he was not in favour of the new measures, which has made these gentlemen happy. One perceives that England has not been so excited since the Reform Bill which also turned this country upside down.

with books and writing kit on it. Above the fireplace is the portrait of George III on his horse which has been moved to this room from the vestibule. It is a pity that Lili chose to paint the room from this particular angle, as she has had to omit its most spectacular feature, since she was sitting on it, which was a magnificent four-poster bed, with gilded wood posts and rococo cornice surmounted by the family crest and furnished with the same material as the curtains, similarly bunched and swagged.

With us, this room was sometimes used as a store-room and sometimes as a staff bedroom (most of the staff wing being uninhabitable). At one point it housed two nubile Italian girls called Rina and Pina, with minimal English and exotic jerseys, who attempted to keep the house running in between high-pitched conversations about their boyfriends. Their younger sister, disappointingly called Francesca, worked for my grandmother at the other end of the village until she went berserk and chased her employer round the kitchen table with a carving knife.

WILLY'S ROOM   FEBRUARY 1846

LILI'S STAY AT AYNHOE SEEMED TO BE COMING TO AN END, AS Sir Thomas was embarrassed at continuing to live off William Ralph and planned a series of visits for them all to various relatives to live off them instead. Lili was consumed with worry about Willy. His illness, whatever it was, had returned and his Oxford entrance examination was postponed for yet another year, to his mother's dismay. After a miserable winter Lili's spirits were at a low ebb. Her patience with the tedious social round of acquaintances and distant relatives was sorely stretched and her tart observations on the unfortunate Lady Chetwynd, among others, were perhaps a fortunate safety valve.

16 FEBRUARY 1846

Lady Chetwynd is truly the least interesting woman that I have ever seen, stiff, cold, stupid, not to mince words. The daughters take after their mother, but their reserve can be attributed to their 18 years, which is quite appropriate.

WILLY'S ROOM, FEBRUARY 1846

I cannot identify this room with certainty, but it is on the south side of the house on the second floor. It looks over the top of the cedar tree which still stands on the lawn. For once, Lili shows a member of the family *in situ*. Her son Willy is reading a book and beside him on the table are several more. Perhaps he was still going through the motions of attempting to get into Balliol when she started the painting, although on the date she completed it he was well aware that his father had decided that he was to travel in Italy for the sake of his health. Willy looks very comfortable, with a warm fire and his feet against the fender. He wears striped trousers and what was probably a smoking jacket with turned-back cuffs. His formal frock coat, with his top hat and walking stick, lies ready on the bed.

The room's large rug appears to match the wallpaper or at least comes very close to it. The striped loose covers may look a bit depressed, but with its bookcases, its velvet-covered table and its comfortable chairs, it looks a most congenial room. The splendid four-poster bed has disappeared, along with all the other ones in the house at that time. It seems that they were all sold by my great-aunt Roma, Willy's unmarried daughter who looked after him in his old age, as she thought they were unhygienic. (Admittedly, they were probably full of woodworm by the end of the century.) She bought a quantity of brass bedsteads to replace

Willy, aged about fourteen. Watercolour drawing by a friend of Sir Thomas and Lili. All the paintings of Willy as a child show him with his mouth open. Later on, any tendency towards an adenoidal gape was hidden by a beard.

18 OCTOBER 1845

Willy and Aubrey Cartwright went foxhunting today. They killed the fox at Shelswell; Aubrey had a fall from his horse on account of which he had to stop and return home with a big bruise on his foot, and Willy pinched his finger opening a gate and brought back a nail all black and blue; if he never has any other accidents than the one he suffered today, we would judge ourselves very happy. I can see him developing a true English taste....

A fine ink drawing of Sir Thomas (left) and Richard Aubrey foxhunting. In Julia's scrapbook and undoubtedly painted by a guest – possibly Sir William Ross, who was a frequent visitor.

18 FEBRUARY 1846

Cart. is acting in this affair after having the advice of the doctor and he himself is quite ready to send Willy to Italy and Willy is even more ready to follow his counsel joyfully; he much prefers Italy to England which upsets me very much and makes me very concerned for his future. He will spend his life in idleness, without aim, without profession, and this lack of occupation will throw him into dangerous company, and will lead him into habits which will spoil him for the rest of his life. Willy's future is a subject of great concern to me, and I tremble to think of it.

them, some of which afflict us yet. The curtains and bed hangings are of a matching white material. The bookcases are built in and, judging by the style of the handles, had been put there recently. They had probably been installed at William Ralph's request by one of the village carpenters, perhaps one of the Secull or Walton families whose trade this was. One of the drawers is open and there are curtains covering the shelves below.

I think the curious piece of tiered furniture between the windows is meant to have a flat top, although it could have been a baize-covered writing slope since there are letters on it and Lili's perspective could still let her down occasionally. If it is a writing slope, it is certainly a very peculiar shape.

The bell-pull would have connected by a complicated series of wires to a bell with a curled spring on a board with many others in the passage in the servants' wing. Doubtless there were bell-pulls of a similar pattern throughout the house – this one is of the same design as that in the pink bedroom and one in a picture that Lili painted of the sitting room in the Rectory next door, where Stephen was Rector.

TOMMY'S ROOM   FEBRUARY 1846

WHILE LILI FRETTED CEASELESSLY OVER WILLY, HER attitude to Tommy was always relaxed to the point of nonchalance. He seems to have rewarded her with a correspondingly robust and sanguine temperament, perfectly suited to the life of a country gentleman.

Tommy's bedroom is on the top floor in the middle of the house and a corner of the stable wing can be seen through the window. The bed hangings and the curtains are made of the same material as in Willy's room. This was the nursery floor and it seems likely that all these rooms were similarly decorated for that purpose during Soane's alterations

21 FEBRUARY 1846

[Willy's] future seems to me to have a very distressing appearance. May God will that it turns out differently. Tommy has been out hunting today and the run went well. Tommy enjoyed himself wonderfully well; the fox led the whole troupe as far as Edgecott where they lost it beyond hope of refinding it.

before 1805. Julia's paintings of the bedroom belonging to her youngest daughters, Fanny and Julia, and only recently vacated by them since their marriages, had similar material on the twin four-poster beds. The wallpaper may have been renewed, since it has a pattern of small sprigs of flowers of a type which was fashionable at this time, but the fitted carpet, which does not match it, would have been original.

When we lived at Aynhoe there was only one area of fitted carpet in the whole of the house, and this covered the floors of my parents' bedroom, sitting room and dressing room. Elsewhere, there were floating islands of carpet in seas of polished boards of varying quality, and ageing runners in the corridors. Fortunately, my grandfather brought back from Persia some fine rugs. Sir Fairfax spent some years there in the 1880s as First Secretary to the British Legation and several of them were made for him. These rugs enabled my parents to make the public rooms rather more friendly than they might have been otherwise when the house first opened. The rugs are mostly still with us, although showing the strain of having had ten thousand pairs of feet over them each year.

Tommy's bedroom has a comfortable armchair with a cotton dust-cover. A few of these dust-covers still survive, though the remains of some have been relegated to dusters, their patterns faded but still recognizable. Tommy has only two books on his table, unlike his brother, which indicates the difference in their characters. He was less intellectual and more outgoing than Willy. His health was never a

8 OCTOBER 1846

All our gentlemen went shooting today at Great Tew and they had an excellent shoot from which they did not return until eight o'clock in the evening. Our ladies went to lunch at Tew and I would have done likewise if I had not been indisposed. The weather was favourable enough. This evening Henry's advancement to the rank of Colonel was celebrated by a Ball for the servants in which the young people of our circle took part, despite the weariness caused to them by the long shoot at Tew. Tommy has amused himself a great deal throughout this day.

Ink sketch of the men of the family netting birds in a marsh around 1820, assisted by a setter. From Julia's scrapbook.

TOMMY'S ROOM, FEBRUARY 1846

19 FEBRUARY 1846

Willy left this morning for London, from where he will not be returning until the day after tomorrow. I am preparing myself for the worst, for his departure for Italy, and Cart. is counting on him establishing himself there for two years in order to establish his health fully. This coming separation and all the dangers attached to this stay in a foreign land upset me very much. I have spent the morning packing up my books, for our departure from Aynhoe is approaching.

problem and he was good at shooting and the other country sports so much admired at the time. On the table is something that looks like a cartridge bag which had escaped from the gun room, wherever that may have been.

All the remaining chairs in the room have cane seats. The pair at the far end appear to be lacquered in black in the Regency manner, and beyond the bed, only partially visible, is a fine Chinese Chippendale chair which we still have. I wonder why it was relegated to the obscurity of a nursery bedroom. In the centre of the room is a basket containing a small dog. This was Julia's own pet, often appearing in her paintings, but it seems to have started to follow Lili around companionably as she painted.

This was the last painting of Aynhoe for several months, since Lili and her husband went to stay with a succession of family and friends while their future accommodation in Sweden was so uncertain. Tommy and his tutor were staying with Stephen at the Rectory and Willy was off to Italy. Lili did not return until August.

Tommy, aged about ten. A companion portrait by a family to the one of Willy on page 71. Tommy, as ever, looking tidy and self-contained.

STEPHEN'S DRAWING ROOM (THE RECTORY, AYNHO)

5 AUGUST 1846

MUCH HAD HAPPENED BETWEEN THE DAY WHEN LILI outlined the plan for the boys and their tutor to stay with Stephen at the Rectory and this painting of Stephen's drawing room. Lili and Sir Thomas spent most of March in London, and April with Mary and Henry Gunning in the Rectory at Wigan. It became clear that Sir Thomas was not going to be offered another diplomatic post in the foreseeable future and that they would be staying in Stockholm for a few more years. There was no certainty of obtaining a house there and their previous establishment had been taken back by the landlord. In May they returned to London, where Lili became involved in society again, and where she was indignant to

23 FEBRUARY 1846

The morning was spent packing, and we left Aynhoe at two o'clock to our great sorrow. Willy and Tommy as well as Mr. Algar are going to establish themselves with Stephen where they will spend some weeks, until the time when our future projects develop and can be put into execution.

receive a letter from Stephen asking for £60 to cover the weeks that Tommy and his tutor had spent with him.

More devastating disagreements followed, however. Sir Thomas had been getting steadily more bad-tempered, and eventually confessed that he had been thinking of retiring from the Diplomatic Service. This, combined with the uncertainties regarding where they would live if he returned to Sweden, led to a row with Lili which upset her a good deal. The days during which Lili worked on this painting had therefore been full of incident and considerable pain, though her husband had now pardoned her for his bad temper.

Stephen and Frederick were the two churchmen in the family, although Julia and May (Mary Catherine) had also married into the church. On Lili's visits to their houses she had painted their drawing rooms in the same album. When she returned to Aynhoe, she started on a short series of interiors of other houses in the village, starting with Stephen's drawing room. The Rectory is immediately beside the Park house, divided from it by a narrow cobbled road which was once the front drive to the main house. At that time the Rectory was a fairly large rambling house, but it has been reduced in recent years to a less uncomfortable shape and size and is no longer in ecclesiastical occupation.

28 JULY 1846

The post brought us bad news from Stockholm; Mr. Gordon finds neither house nor apartment and Cart., to be able to arrange this affair somehow, proposed to return to Sweden around the 20th August. He will take himself there alone, and as for me, I shall await, either in England or wherever it is planned for me to await, the circumstances and events which will allow me to rejoin him. Tommy will spend, to all appearances, the next winter in Geneva. All these projects, the separations, occupy and preoccupy me a great deal . . .

Julia, as his mother-in-law, could paint Stephen's bedroom at the Rectory, whereas it might have been considered to be improper for Lili to do so. Watercolour from Julia's volume of interiors.

[76]

30 JULY 1846

On our arrival here we found a letter from Mr. Cart. to Cart. in which he blames him for wanting to leave me alone here when he leaves for Sweden; this letter has put him in a very bad temper, and I spent my evening and my night in tears. Alas, what's to be done? I have truly at heart to be obedient in everything but there is great difficulty in always putting up with the mortification without resisting and certainly this evening things were said to me that have upset me very much and which have really turned me upside down. May God give me the grace to forget them, for I forgive them as I myself wish to be forgiven.

The drawing room looks out over the garden through a large bow window. Through it the garden can be seen, with its neat gravel path round the edge and the round islands of flowerbeds in a sea of lawn, filled with brilliantly coloured bedding-out plants and typical of the period. It is a style which is now nearly extinct, but still to be seen in public parks, especially at the seaside. The plain, heavy curtains give some relief from the dizzy flower patterns on the wallpaper, chair covers and carpet. As well as having the velvet curtains and the lace ones which are hooked back and which hang from wooden rings on a curved rail, there are blinds on the window which can be pulled down with red silk cords. These match the bell-pull by the fireplace, and are similar to the ones in the Park house. Could there have been a shop in Banbury where these were ordered by the dozen?

The furniture appears to have been purchased within the last few years, judging by the style. As a younger son of this large family, Stephen would have been unlikely to have been given much furniture from the house, especially when one considers how full of guests it always was. The large armchair in the centre of the room, however, looks suspiciously like one in the drawing room at the Park. There are a few ornaments around the room and not many pictures. It looks like what it was – a bachelor's room. No doubt he had neither the time nor the inclination to collect the numerous objects that were then fashionable. There are books on his table and a letter and its envelope which has a seal and a red border. Since Lili spent so long in Stephen's drawing room, I suppose she had forgiven him for his letter. However, Stephen was never very popular with the rest of the family. After his death, he was succeeded at the Rectory by his brother Freddy, who was in turn succeeded by Henry's son, William Digby Cartwright.

To the left is a fine harmonium with two manuals with the music ready above. Could it be the hymns for next Sunday's service? On the desk, beside the book and the two

3 AUGUST 1846

We have been given the details of a terrible storm which broke over London on Saturday evening. The results are serious. In the Palace alone, the broken windows are valued at £2,000. The week-end has suffered from hail above all. The weather has changed and although it is warm and heavy, we have tons of rain which does not refresh the air.

Stephen's unpopularity with the rest of the family is shown in this caricature of him by an unknown hand in Cornwallis's scrapbook.

[77]

STEPHEN'S DRAWING ROOM AT THE RECTORY, AYNHO, 5 AUGUST 1846

26 AUGUST 1846

Cart. left early this morning, wanting to be in London by three o'clock. I took my leave of him in tears, not knowing when I will see him again. We went to dine and spend the night at North Aston where many people are gathered at the moment. I was not very carefree and very much disposed to amuse myself and the evening seemed very long to me. I talked with Mrs. Henry Goulbourn, a woman very ill in body and mind, and who is completely demented at times.

boxes, is a tobacco jar with a lid, which suggests that Stephen smoked a pipe, unless it was a piece of standard equipment, as in most houses, with tobacco available for guests.

The room itself has been enlarged to accommodate the bow window. Lili shows the panes of the window as being rectangular in shape and longer horizontally than vertically, which is unusual. Whether this really was the case or whether Lili has got into difficulties with perspective again, leaving herself without enough height for the window panes, is difficult to ascertain. At any rate, the window must have been put there in order to obtain more light. Despite this, I still remember this room as being rather dark, on the rare occasions when I was in it as a child. At that time the Rector was rather gloomy and inclined to irritation at our unauthorized trips up the church tower, since we knew where the key was kept, so we tended to avoid him. However, I remember visiting the garden by invitation earlier on, not long after the war, and finding it had gone wild, its only decorations being a summer-house and a goat.

MRS JONES' COTTAGE 25 AUGUST 1846

IN THE SUMMER OF 1846 SIR THOMAS RETURNED TO SWEDEN. He had refused to let Lili come with him, despite her entreaties, on the grounds that they had no certain knowledge of where they would be living. She disliked being landed on the family and dependent on them. She had very little money and was perpetually trying to economize. Sir Thomas was finding his salary so inadequate that he had had to ask his father to finance their trip to England in the first place. (Despite this, he had bought three hunters for his sons and himself and a carriage during the course of the winter.) Lili resigned herself to her situation with her usual good sense and remained at Aynhoe, feeling a little like abandoned luggage.

25 AUGUST 1846

If I must stay here, I will keep myself occupied from morning to night so that the time passes quickly. I will certainly not mope about staying here and meanwhile have a heavy heart to think that in that case I will be separated from Cart. for six to eight months. May God's will be done in everything.

This was the first of Lili's pictures of cottage interiors. I cannot identify it with certainty, although it is one of the larger cottages judging by the size of the room. On a pencilled note below the picture Lili wrote at some later date that it was 'Willy's study in the cottage'. Whichever house it was, Willy must have used it when Aynhoe Park was let during the period when he was MP for Oxfordshire from 1868 to 1885. The lattice window is of the seventeenth century and the panelling is from a similar date or a little later. The stone fireplace, with its iron grate, is of good quality and a kettle is keeping warm on the hob on the left. Lili had made several visits to cottagers with Julia previously and on this occasion they both painted pictures of the same room. Julia made her own painting from the position of the chair beyond the little table and looking towards the window.

This painting conveys a sad and lonely impression of the old lady, sitting close by her fire in a sparsely furnished room. Perhaps, too, some of Lili's own feelings of loneliness and isolation, abandoned as she was once again by her husband and Willy for an unknown length of time, have been transmitted into the picture along with her sympathetic

Julia's painting of Mrs. Jones' cottage was done on the same day as Lili's painting of the same room.

MRS JONES' COTTAGE, 25 AUGUST 1846

observation of their hostess. I have the impression that Mrs Jones is a widow and that all but the essentials have been sold from her parlour. There is not one rug on the wide old floorboards and there are no curtains. The part of the room that is visible contains only four chairs. The old lady seems to be sitting patiently, looking at nothing in particular, although in reality she may have been asked to pose like this, as she has her knitting which, with its ball of blue wool, is on the table, and she would normally have been occupied with it while she talked with her visitors. In Julia's painting she sits with her back to Julia, which would have been unthinkable otherwise. Also on the table are a workbox, a book (probably a Bible) and a pewter mug. Mrs Jones is dressed in a simple blue dress with an apron over it and a white shawl. On her head is a white mob cap.

The chairs have rush seats and two of them have blue cushions similar to the ones in Mrs Page's room. The bellows hang by the fire and on the mantelpiece stands a tobacco jar and a candle. The overall impression is of a room in a house which was built for more prosperous inhabitants.

THE INFANTS' SCHOOL   27 AUGUST 1846

BENEATH THIS PICTURE LILI PENCILLED IN AT A LATER DATE that this room became 'Willy's sitting room at the cottage'. But since she wrote that his study was in the cottage occupied by Mrs Jones and that his dining room was in Mrs Page's cottage this is rather confusing. At any rate, in 1846 this room was used as the infants' school and looks well established as such. It is possible that some of the infants attended the huge children's party given by Lili's sister-in-law, Sophie Willes, two miles away at Astrop.

As in the upper school, the fireplace is in the corner of the room, this time protected from childish investigations by a large guard. The great tiered bench takes up most of one wall. Presumably the children sat there for most of their lessons, as there are only two chairs around the room. These are of the same type as those in Mrs Page's sitting room, high ladderback chairs with rush seats, cheap, practical and easy to replace. The sturdy table has a book on it, open and ready for the lesson, with the blackboard pointer laid across it, and near by a Bible, a pot full of quill pens and the school bell.

At the back of the room, looking very ornate in such a plain setting, is the harmonium, on a stand with rather fragile-looking legs. Round the walls are pictures, several framed in glass and passe-partout, which look as if they were put up in a great hurry as they hang randomly at different heights. The cow, the donkey and the elephant look as if they might be coloured prints. An alphabet hangs on the wall by the window, but what is the purpose of the curious diagram below it, looking as if it is composed of horizontal and vertical bars in black and white? There is a text propped up by the wall and a long list of words on the easel. Over the fireplace hangs something that looks like a certificate, perhaps the qualifications of the teacher or the record of a prize won by the school. On the mantelpiece there is a vase of flowers and something which might be a hearth brush, but could equally be a switch used for the disciplining of naughty children.

5 AUGUST 1846

The party was given at Astrop today, and we went there at three o'clock. 212 children with their parents were regaled with tea and cakes, and following this treat, the donkey racing began and many games which greatly excited the assembled company. The spectators there comprised about 500 people, and as the weather was fine, the party lasted until the evening.

THE INFANTS' SCHOOL, 27 AUGUST 1846

MRS PAGE'S COTTAGE, 7 SEPTEMBER 1846

MRS PAGE'S COTTAGE   7 SEPTEMBER 1846

1 SEPTEMBER 1846

Mrs. Cart. and I walked, rather naïvely, on the new railway on which work is taking place, and we found ourselves surrounded by wagons, workman's horses, masons and machinery in a manner very disagreeable to ladies.

LILI RETAINED HER ENTHUSIASM FOR LOCAL AFFAIRS AND shared the family's interest in the progress of the Oxford to Banbury section of the railway line. This proceeded at a snail's pace and with maximum devastation of the local countryside a mile from Aynho, much like the current motorway workings which are parallel to the railway and even closer to the village. She was always fascinated by other people's houses, great and small, and her reflections on the lack of progress of the work at Great Tew strike a contemporary note. Great Tew was sold in 1987 with all its original contents, after the death of Matthew Boulton's descendant, Eustace Robb.

This picture has a pencilled note by Lili stating that this room was

3 SEPTEMBER 1846

Julia and Ansey went to Great Tew, which they found full of workmen. Mr Boulton's building works barely move, and if Fanny and her husband arrive in the autumn, they will find their house and their great library totally unready to receive them.

Print of the building of the railway from Julia's scrapbook. The navvies poached relentlessly. They beat up Milward, the gamekeeper, causing William Ralph to forbid the ladies of the household to go for long walks.

'Willy's dining room in the cottage', making it clear that Mrs Page and Mrs Jones lived in different parts of the same house.

The windows are seventeenth-century in character and the stone fireplace is of good quality. The room gives the impression of being used as a parlour, kitchen and dining room. While there are no curtains or rugs other than the mat in front of the hearth, the floor consisting of rough stone flags, the room gives a comfortable impression, perhaps because of the friendly-looking set of Windsor chairs and the bird in its cage.

Mrs Page looked after the hens, according to Lili's diary of a few months later when she recorded that the unfortunate woman had just died of dropsy. That is, assuming that it was the same Mrs Page. However, in this painting she looks relatively young and not at all dropsical. She wears a cheerful-looking shawl. Her little table is quite elegant, with its reeded column and tripod legs. On it sit her bonnet, with its ribbons hanging down, and her workbox and knitting. She has just begun to knit something in blue wool which is already on the needles, but there are two balls of red wool ready for use. There appears to be a large pair of socks on the table, perhaps waiting to be mended.

The dresser is full of china. There are four large plates and eight smaller plates or bowls, several big dishes of a different set, some copper jugs and a few glasses. The cutlery box stands below on the cupboard. The dining table was probably the drop-leaved one between the windows, as it could be easily set up. On it is a tray, a wooden butter bowl and a bottle. A curious map of the world, in two halves, hangs above it, perhaps a legacy from the contents of the school. There is a ladderback chair with a blue cushion. The imposing mantelpiece, with its carved wooden framing above, has three keys and a pair of toasting forks hanging from it. The stand for an iron hangs to the left and there is a selection of ornaments to the right.

23 SEPTEMBER 1846

The post brought me a letter from Cart. also from Copenhagen, where he arrived in a hurricane which prevented him from embarking on a Norwegian vessel for Gothenburg. He was expecting to leave the next day to go by and to rejoin the Nowkoping boat; I think he will arrive next Sunday in Stockholm.

THE CHURCH   16 SEPTEMBER 1846

THE OCCUPATION OF THE VILLAGE IN THE CIVIL WAR, FIRST by the Parliamentarians and then, for a year, by the Royalists, had left Aynho church badly damaged. It was demolished in 1723 and rebuilt in the classical style to match the Park house next door, with pediments and high, arched windows. Its architect, Edward Wing, was involved in the building of several London churches and Lili's painting shows how much the interior resembles a city church rather than a country one. The first Thomas Cartwright helped financially with the rebuilding and sent Wing, his master mason, who had been in charge of the rebuilding of the house some twenty years earlier, to assist with the work. A nineteenth-century letter in the archives describes it as resembling 'more a gentleman's stables than a church'.

As a Catholic, Lili was a less frequent visitor than the rest of the family to this church where Stephen was Rector. Both her sons had been christened there as Protestants when their visits to England had made this possible. However they had been already been baptized in Frankfurt in the Catholic manner a few days after birth. Lili, whose religious attitudes were more tolerant than those about her, would sometimes join the family in the church for prayers but not for services. Her difficulty lay in getting to Mass, either in the little Catholic chapel at the village of Hethe, some six miles away, or in Banbury. Her diary for the early part of this visit is full of references to this problem. She had to be driven by a member of the family or not go at all, as it was unthinkable that the carriage should be taken out on a Sunday, that being the day of rest for the coachman and, perhaps as importantly, for the carriage horses.

The span of the church roof is very great and it is unsupported by pillars (a condition which has led to problems in the recent past) and

31 AUGUST 1845

The annoying aspect of Aynhoe made itself felt today: that is the lack of a chapel. Since I was here last, one has been built at Banbury but it is still six miles from Aynhoe and the distance is too great to walk. To take the carriage out is too much of an inconvenience and quite against the custom [on a Sunday], and I have no desire to impose. But one day when a railway is built from Oxford to Banbury I will be able to get there easily, for it is only a mile and a half to reach the station, which will be at Clifton, from where it will take me a quarter of an hour to Banbury. What a good thing it will be for me when they build this railway line.

8 SEPTEMBER 1846

I spent my morning drawing the interior of the church, a church of little interest, for its architecture is altogether in bad taste.

THE CHURCH, 16 SEPTEMBER 1846

Another, better painted watercolour of the church by Lili which Julia put into her own book of interiors.

28 OCTOBER 1845

Julia and I went to Banbury. The weather was very fine. I went into the chapel for a moment to say my prayers and from there we went to see the garden of Mr. Perry, a very competent gardener, who owns a nursery garden at the gates of Banbury. Perry is a Catholic. He is one of the main-stays of the Catholic Church in Banbury and he spoke very highly of Fr. Tandy who I would greatly like to get to know a little before going to him for Confession. It is impossible to permit him to come and see me in this house; I can only act little by little, and by going often to Banbury find the occasion and means to get to know him.

there is no chancel. The box pews by the chapel on the right and those below the pulpit were for the choir. The hymn books and prayer books lie on the tops of the rest of the pews. The large windows have clear glass in them and those on the south side have curtains against the sun. The floor is stone-flagged and very rough. The organ was introduced in 1835, an event which Lili records in her diary. Around the church are memorials to members of the family and others and on either side of the altar are the coats of arms of Richard Cartwright and his wife, Mary Egerton. The recess on the left is the vestry and that on the right is the Cartwright family chapel, most of it inconveniently occupied by the florid tomb in black marble of Richard Cartwright, founder of the family at Aynhoe. His corpse, along with those of the rest of the early members of the family, was interred in the vault under the lawn outside the church door. When it was full, by the end of the eighteenth century, the family were buried near by. Lili may not have worshipped with the others but she was buried alongside them and she lies there now, under a complicated piece of ironwork which looks simultaneously continental and Catholic.

My brother and I were brought up as Catholics and we would go to Mass every Sunday at the little chapel in Souldern, at the other end of the park. It had been charmingly decorated by Italian prisoners of war a

25 FEBRUARY 1846

Today being Ash Wednesday, I particularly wanted to attend Mass at Weedon as they have a priest there who reads the Office, but Mass is said in an Inn and it was not felt to be suitable for me to go; so I said a prayer at home.

few years earlier. We would be taken there by my Italian grandmother and driven in her ponderous Humber by her erratic chauffeur, Jaycock. My non-driving grandmother would sit completely relaxed, interrogating us about our activities, while we whisked round blind corners on the wrong side of the A41 at around sixty miles an hour.

MRS HANCOCK'S COTTAGE, AN ALMSHOUSE
24 SEPTEMBER 1846

BY NOW LILI HAD SETTLED BACK INTO THE ROUTINE AT Aynhoe. She spent much time with her mother-in-law, visiting the neighbours, entertaining guests, calling on the cottagers and finding out what was going on in the village. In a way, she was serving an apprenticeship in how the mistress of the house went about her business. This was not so different from her mother's activities at Sandizell, but it served to introduce Lili to many more people in the village and to make her acquainted with their problems. William Ralph was now fully retired but the house was just as busy with visiting members of the family. Lili filled the intervals between letters from Sir Thomas (in Stockholm) and from Willy (in Naples) with painting.

The almshouses at the northern end of the village were built in 1821 by the trustees of the estate of John Baker, a successful Oxford glazier who had left a substantial sum for the purpose. Built in a long row, they have great charm and veteran inhabitants of Aynho at that period would have been fortunate to spend their old age in them, as they still do. Each house, small as it is, has a little garden to the south. In the picture, it can be seen that Mrs Hancock has chosen to plant irises and some red flowers by the path, with a border of small grey plants at the edge. At the end of the garden is a wall topped with high railings which protect the almshouse gardens from the field beyond.

17 SEPTEMBER 1846

Today there was a cricket match between Aynhoe and Astrop; Aynhoe lost the game; all our gentlemen took part there. Lord Bowles and his son dined here. This morning I wrote to Cart. and to Willy. This was the fourth letter that I have dispatched to Stockholm.

22 SEPTEMBER 1846

We have all been to Banbury to see the distribution of the prizes which are given annually to the farmers and agriculturalists who have distinguished themselves in their conduct and their success in agriculture. A great dinner followed the distribution of the prizes, in which many of the neighbours joined. The Aynhoe men who hoped to get some prizes did not have that satisfaction. Others even more ancient in their service than them carried them off over the Aynhoites.

Mrs Hancock's Cottage, an Almshouse, 24 September 1846

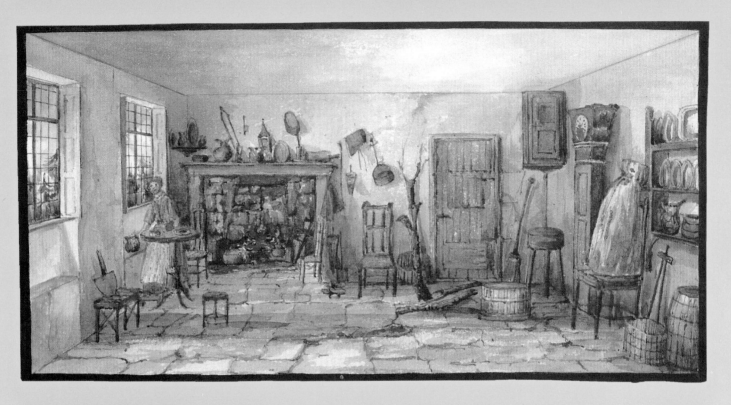

MRS WATTS' COTTAGE, CALLED THE PEST HOUSE, 5 OCTOBER 1846

23 SEPTEMBER 1846

Tonight we had a storm which gave us a rainy day. The post arrived very late after midday and the cause of this lateness has been assigned to the thunderbolt which struck the engine and damaged it. We do not know whether or not this rumour is true.

When I was a child, the barn seen in the distance belonged to Mr Oakey, whose family still farm in the village. I was taught to milk a cow in this barn by the cowman, Les, when I was about seven years old, which was a more satisfying and entertaining experience for me than for the cow. At that time there was no automatic milking machinery, and buckets for the Oakey family's milk were carried up the cobbled pavement of the main road on wooden yokes, a practice that ceased soon afterwards. My brother and I would also watch the rat hunts in Mr Watts' stackyard across the road from the almshouses, where the rats emerged from the straw to be set on by terriers.

Trees can be seen beyond the garden. These are growing in the garden of the Grammar House where my grandparents lived, but which was still in use as a grammar school when the picture was painted.

Mrs Hancock is sitting at her little table having a meal. There is a neat white tablecloth and on it a loaf of bread, an earthenware pot, perhaps for a stew, and a plate with some food. She has a jug in her hand, ready to pour. The old lady wears a charming little cap of lace, with blue ribbons, and has a lace collar above her neat dark blue-grey dress. Her poke bonnet for wearing out of doors hangs behind the window. She wears no shawl although the door to the garden is wide open, so perhaps Lili started this painting at the beginning of the week, when she remarks on the magnificence of the weather. Mrs Hancock's fire burns brightly and although the room is simply furnished, the impression is of a cottage where the old lady is reasonably comfortable and well cared for.

The kettle is on the hob, ready for the inevitable cups of tea, and there are the usual pothooks by the fireplace. Beside the glasses on the mantelpiece is a small vase, with flowers picked, no doubt, from her own borders, and her chinaware is stacked on the set of shelves behind her. Mrs Hancock has changed into her indoor shoes when she came in from the garden and her pattens, with their raised wooden soles, lie by the garden door on the mat. Her basket hangs on the wall behind her. The chairs are of the usual cottage pattern but she has put thin cushions over their rush seats. She sits on the fourth chair, wearing her striped cotton apron, and has wisely put her feet up on a small footstool to keep them off the cold and damp of the flagstones.

5 SEPTEMBER 1846

The weather continues to be superb; the harvest is all gathered in; only the potatoes are lacking this year in England and in Ireland, which is for this poor Ireland, otherwise so unhappy, a surfeit of affliction.

MRS WATTS' COTTAGE, CALLED THE PEST HOUSE
1 OCTOBER 1846

THE COTTAGE KNOWN AS THE PEST HOUSE, DEEP IN THE Pestwood near Croughton, was pulled down at the beginning of this century as it was in a semi-ruinous condition. I never saw it, as it had disappeared long before I rode through the woods on my pony to look at the bluebells. Its name derived from its use as a house for isolating patients from the village who were suffering from infectious diseases, particularly smallpox. It was thought to be built on very ancient foundations. It seems that Lili made her sketch during her visit to the cottage and worked it up later. The haste in which she did the sketch is apparent, since there is little of her usual meticulous detail.

In Lili's painting, Mrs Watts is standing by the window behind her little tripod table holding a large copper jug. She wears a blue dress and a full-length apron. The room looks unkempt because of the branches which have been collected from the woods around the house but have not yet been cut up. The huge fireplace has a fire which heats up the various copper pots for a meal. Mrs Watts' pattens lie at the hearth. It is a large room with rough stone flags which look very old. A shovel stands between the windows, probably for removing the ash from the fire. It is clear that Mrs Watts is a washerwoman and there are several large containers which look like half-barrels or washing tubs. There is a large sack on the chair to the right which could contain the washing, perhaps to be carried the mile from the village and to be taken back clean over the fields. There would have been nothing romantic about the harsh realities of her life.

There is only one ornament amongst the household china around the room, a ship in a bottle on the right-hand end of the mantelpiece. The door looks much repaired and the grandfather clock appears to have lost its top. I have the impression that Mrs Watts is very poor and hard-working, bravely able to cope with a harsh existence in difficult times. How great a contrast there is between her solitary cottage wash house and the great laundry at Aynhoe.

1 OCTOBER 1846

Mr. Algar left this morning to spend some days with his family, which gave me the opportunity to occupy Tommy more with his French and his German which he reads daily with me. We went for a walk together, and I have been drawing the cottage which is known here by the name of the Pest House. It is situated at the bottom of a charming little wood.

THE SCHOOL   13 OCTOBER 1846

19 SEPTEMBER 1846

*I spent my morning drawing the
Great Room of the school, which
has a vaulted roof full of
interlaced beams, which gave
me immense trouble to depict.
In occupying myself daily with
my drawing, my reading and my
correspondence, I find the
means of passing my time very
rapidly.*

THERE WERE THREE SCHOOL BUILDINGS IN THE VILLAGE: THE
Grammar School, which became my grandparents' house,
the Infants' School and the Upper School, which is shown
here. This painting, perhaps the best and most complex of
them all, had caused Lili much difficulty and she had spent the better
part of three weeks struggling with it. Her drawing of the beams of the
school roof is a triumph by any standards and particularly so in view of
her problems with perspective. Her youngest sister-in-law, Julia, now
married to the much-disliked Edward Goulbourn, had been the governor
of the school, though whether this was official or unofficial is not known,
and there is a copy in her scrapbook of the effusive eulogy to her work
which was sung to her by the children before her wedding. Within a year
Lili herself was to take on this role.

The schoolroom is high and proportionately wide and there are two
long beams across the middle to support the roof. The fireplace is
between the two sets of tiered benches with their panelled boards, and it
is unused. A desk has been pushed into it out of the way and it is used as a
storage area for baskets, books and any items which need to be easily
available. Perhaps the stove was brought out for use once the weather
started to be cold enough. So far, this particular October had only been
wet. The benches round the room are of a suitable height for children.
On the right-hand wall are two side tables for written work, their pots of
ink ready for use. The harmonium stands between them, no doubt used
by the teacher to instil suitable hymns into the pupils. There are four big
easels and one of them holds a blackboard which has something
indecipherable about God written on it. The central easel has lists of
simple words in capital letters on it for reading practice. Although this
was the senior school, the level of reading was very low by our standards,
though probably better than the majority of other village schools as it

26 SEPTEMBER 1846

*I spent nearly all the day in the
big school where I am doing the
interior. The very complicated
ceiling of beams is giving us
great difficulty. Mrs. Cart. is
occupied with the same work.
This evening I received a letter
from Miss Gordon which gives
me the fullest details about the
death of our poor little friend
Lady Augusta Bondi. She died in
childbirth, leaving her husband
inconsolable and the father of a
little girl. Mr. and Mrs. Bisley
and Mr. and Mrs. Leonard dined
here.*

THE SCHOOL, 13 OCTOBER 1846

[97]

Ink drawing by Nattes of the White Hart Inn in the centre of the village. Nattes filled an album with sketches of the Park house, the village and the surrounding area in 1815.

had an excellent reputation. The Grammar School, mostly patronized by the sons of local farmers, had a poor reputation and few pupils, which led to its closure in the 1880s.

Two Windsor chairs stand by the fireplace recess on a little rug and look as if they were intended for the teachers. There are religious inscriptions everywhere, which is not surprising as this was a Church of England school. Over the two windows are written 'Pray to God' and 'Do not steal' respectively. Of the other inscriptions around the walls I can find 'The Lord you must always obey', 'Feed my Lambs', 'Remain faithful to the Commandments' and 'Fear ye God'. There are other inscriptions and texts, each one framed in black and with a small cross or rosette at the top. No doubt Stephen, as the Rector, had a hand in this formidable array of injunctions.

The end wall is of dressed stone, but the area below the beams may have been rendered to keep out the damp. A picture of Christ and two other religious paintings hang in the centre of the chimney, surrounded by texts. Above one of the maps on the wall to the left is the plain and serviceable clock, which was doubtless watched surreptitiously by the children as the end of the school day approached.

I never went into the school as a child, though I passed it many times.

It was presided over by the much-respected Mrs Sczepy. The standards of the school were high, and remained so until a few years ago, when the school, like the village shop, closed down. The church and the pub, not necessarily in that order, are the remaining traditional institutions, with the result, as an inhabitant of Aynho pointed out to me recently, that few people walk in the village streets now, as the focal points of village life, other than those two, have gone. In my childhood, and even more in Lili's time, it was full of life.

No wonder Lili took three weeks to paint this interior. The detail is quite extraordinary.

THE GRAPEHOUSES   5 DECEMBER 1846

LILI'S DIARY RECORDS A MONTH OF ANXIETY FOR THE HEALTH of William Ralph. Dr Perrington from London, despite his fee of one hundred guineas, declared that he was unable to do anything for him and that he was on the point of death. The family gathered round and the classic Victorian deathbed scene ensued. To everyone's surprise he recovered almost immediately, although he remained frail. William had written impulsively to Sir Thomas in Sweden, against Lili's advice, to tell him that his father was dying, and it was thought that he was now on his way home unnecessarily and at a most inconvenient time from the diplomatic point of view. As no one could contact him to stop him, letters were sent to Hamburg to try and reach him on his journey to tell him of his father's return to health. Unable to do anything constructive in the situation, Lili went to paint the greenhouses.

The walled gardens lay at the east end of the village and were very large. Adjacent to these lay the house where Blenkowe, the ratcatcher, lived. This became the cottage, known as the bothy, where our own head gardener, Ted Humphris, lived. There was a large enclosed garden where most of the vegetables and flowers were grown, with paths bordered by box and fruit trees. The smaller walled garden contained the

11 NOVEMBER 1846

Mr. Cart. is becoming weaker and the doctors told Mrs. Cart. that they have no hope of saving him. Mr. Cart. is calm and resigned; he has great strength of spirit and many religious feelings which, at this solemn moment, are helping him to withdraw himself from a world in which he has enjoyed a never-ending happiness. . . . Mrs. Cart. is resigned to the fate that awaits her; she is relieved to see Mr. Cart. so calm and happy, and the courage and example of her daughters Mary and Julia in this unhappy moment give her a little strength . . .

THE GRAPEHOUSES, 5 DECEMBER 1846

14 NOVEMBER 1846

I saw Mr. Cart. today, who, having seen all his children, also let me kiss his hand. He said a few things to me and to William concerning Cart. which will certainly touch him. The state of his health has not worsened; on the contrary, the calm that he is enjoying has a beneficial influence on him. He has gained strength since yesterday and the doctors, especially Dr. Perrington, are surprised that he is no weaker. He is only given sustaining drinks, and sleeping has done him the world of good. He certainly has a head on his shoulders since he did not forget anyone, not even the junior servants at Aynhoe. He has made all the arrangements in case of death. His speeches are heart-breaking for Mrs. Cart. and it is still Mr. Cart. who encourages and consoles her in the most distressing time of her life. I know that Cart. will arrive in time to see his father . . .

greenhouses which included the grapehouses. As can be seen in the painting, these were lean-to houses against the high brick wall which faced south. Lili has found an ingenious way of depicting the first one, by ignoring the exterior wall and enabling us to look straight into the interior.

The rear wall has been rendered, as have the benches on the other side. The stone floor looks perfectly clean and tidy. The vines are trained up the joists in regimental perfection and look as if they would not dare put shoots out sideways. The flowerpots are arranged in rows around the edge of the bench and on the shelves above and are impeccably well ordered. The watering cans look as if they might be expected to salute when the head gardener, Mr Brown, came in. No doubt his under-gardeners felt the same. There is a sandpit in the centre and a set of mobile steps at the back. Unfortunately, it is difficult to identify the plants and flowers in this greenhouse. I would particularly like to know what is the fern-like plant without a pot which appears to be climbing off the bench into the watering can below. Also, I wonder how Mr Brown

William Ralph Cartwright in his bedroom. This painting was done by Julia when her husband was unwell and confined to his room a few months before his death.

15 NOVEMBER 1846

Dr. Perrington went back to London this morning and is pleased with the state of his patient. He has no longer lost hope for his recovery and his living for months, perhaps years.

2 DECEMBER 1846

This morning I received, which is extraordinary, another letter from Cart. of the 20th. He has just received the first news of the illness of Mr. Cart., which has made him beside himself with worry. In a few days I will know if he is expecting to come here or not. In the uncertainty in which I find myself in this regard, I will write as usual tomorrow to Stockholm, Hamburg and Copenhagen.

managed to persuade these vines, and those next door which can be seen through the panes of glass, to produce such splendid quantities of grapes so close to Christmas.

At that time the gardens round the house were well kept, as Lili notes in her diary. William Ralph had remodelled them after the work on the house had finished. He had consulted Humphry Repton briefly on design, but had not taken up his suggestions, perhaps because they might involve redesigning the whole park and the expense would have been great. Instead, he had laid out the garden to the west and the east of the house with walks and flowerbeds, influenced, perhaps by the 'Botanical Magazine' to which he subscribed. More flowerbeds appeared as the fashion of the century changed, and these were serviced from the kitchen garden, which must have been busy enough already producing adequate fruit and vegetables for such an enormous household.

I can just remember the long ranks of box in the big kitchen garden, which was abandoned soon afterwards as it was not possible to keep up such a large area after the war. The small kitchen garden became the centre for the production of plants for the main flowerbeds round the house, which required several thousand annuals. The grapehouses became orchid houses and some of the plants still survive. Little of the garden created by William Ralph remained, after years of occupation by the Army with its Nissen huts and concrete slabs, and the park itself had been one of the largest petrol dumps in the Midlands. My father used the compensation paid by the War Office for the restoration of the house and made economical walls in the garden and the terraces out of the remaining concrete slabs. Like so many things in the country, this temporary arrangement became permanent and the structures remain there still.

Sketch by Lili of the house of Blenkowe, the ratcatcher, in the flower garden, 1828. This house later became the gardener's bothy.

Portrait drawing of Blenkowe, the Aynho ratcatcher, by Sir William Ross. An inscription on the back says that Blenkowe lived to be ninety-three.

THE GREENHOUSE   10 DECEMBER 1846

DURING THE BITTERLY COLD WEATHER, LILI SEEMS TO HAVE found the warmest place in the house for continuing her painting. Although she called it the 'greenhouse', in our day it was known as the orangery or as the Murillo room because of the three large canvases by that artist which were hung there. It bore little resemblance to an orangery, as it had been converted into one of the public rooms somewhat in the manner of a long gallery. It is now the dining room of the Country Households. Built by Thomas Archer, it is at the east end of the house, next to the salon. In Lili's day it must have been well heated by ventilators from the boiler rooms nearby via a series of gratings in the floor. The room is enormous, being two storeys high, and is very light owing to the immense height of the lower windows and the row of smaller windows above. The walls are all trellised and covered with climbing plants. There are cacti in tubs down the side by the windows and a very impressive array of trees and large shrubs in the middle. Two of them are palms of different types. In the foreground and going up the steps is a bank of pot plants of unknown variety. Nearly all the flowers in the room are red.

When I first remember this room, it was piled high with furniture and pictures, as it was one of the rooms retained by my parents as store-rooms when the Army took over the house in 1940. Later we used it occasionally for social events, but more often it was simply a place in which it was possible to enjoy the pictures and furniture on display there in peace and comfort. As the sofas and most of the furniture were Italian, having come to Aynhoe with my Italian grandmother, they tended to be comfortable to curl up on. (The French antique furniture was invariably uncomfortable.) I spent many happy hours in the room, enjoying its contents, with the result that I acquired an enduring interest in Italy and its artefacts.

15 DECEMBER 1846

. . . the cold penetrates everywhere in the houses, which are neither built nor heated as are those in Sweden or in Russia.

THE GREENHOUSE, 10 DECEMBER 1846

THE HOUSEKEEPER'S ROOM, 21 DECEMBER 1846

THE HOUSEKEEPER'S ROOM   21 DECEMBER 1846

4 DECEMBER 1846

The cold continues and encourages foxhunting. These gentlemen have been shooting small game. Tommy, who went to join them after his lessons, killed eleven larks or laverocks which the cold had already made very thin.

LILI WAS BEGINNING TO FIND THE HOUSE VERY COLD, AS THE weather had been consistently icy since late November. It must have been bad for her to mention it at all, used as she was to the arctic corridors and cavernous rooms of Sandizell. William Ralph had recovered enough to spend his days in the schoolroom, no doubt as close to the fire as he could get. Tommy, Henry and Tommy's tutor, Mr Algar, had skated along the canal which ran alongside the new railway all the way to Oxford, some twenty miles away, during the previous week. They all returned by the mail coach the next day. Having run out of the more obvious rooms in the house and deterred by the cold from attempting any more cottage interiors, Lili set about painting the housekeeper's room, which had a suitably efficient fire.

The housekeeper was an important figure in the household, in charge of the china, the linen and all the supplies except the food and the silver. The cook, the butler and the nanny, if any, were the only servants of equal status and power within the household, each with their own subordinates. In many comparable houses memorable power struggles took place between them, but there is no record of whether or not this occurred at Aynhoe.

This room was built by Soane when he linked the servants' wing to the main house, its arched window matching the archway through to the stables on the other side of the courtyard. The stable wing opposite can be seen through the window. A high, dark room, it still looks comfortable and friendly. The wall on the left is panelled but the right-hand wall is lined by the china cupboards and drawers. There is a fine set of late Georgian chairs about the room with blue striped seats. The central table is used as a desk. On it lie the household account books with the pens and inkpot ready for use and behind them a workbox, perhaps for the large amount of mending that must have been required. Two comfortable

16 DECEMBER 1846

The cold continues. Tommy, Henry and Mr. Algar have been skating today as far as Rousham. It is very rare in England to be able to skate the length of six or eight miles.

19 DECEMBER 1946

This morning we have been astonished on getting up to see the most complete thaw. The rain was falling again, and the return of Tommy, of Henry and of Mr. Algar was made by the coach. They arrived this evening, very happy with their expedition. The ice was uneven, which did not stop them making their journey the length of the canal. Henry and Mr. Algar had a small incident of breaking through but after being dried out in a signal box they continued on their way, and arrived at Oxford at six o'clock in the evening.

upholstered chairs stand by the fire. There are several other workboxes about the room and a number of ornaments of glass. The main pictures are unrecognizable family portraits which dominate the room, with a fine flower painting by Monnoyer above the mirror over the fireplace.

The little curtains on the left-hand window screen the room from the staff passage beyond, and the pelmet over the external window looks rather depressing and useless. There are rolls of material in the basket on the left, perhaps for dressmaking. Altogether, it looks like a dark but comfortable working room where much of the organizing of the household would have taken place.

Of the twenty-two people employed in the house, several would have slept in the many rooms of this wing but others would have stayed with their families in the village. When I knew the house this wing was mostly unoccupied, although in later years there were two flats in use on the first floor. We used the housekeeper's room, its cupboards still serving their original purpose, as a tea room for the public when the house was open, the teas being served from our kitchen a little further down the corridor. Before that, we used to have our nursery meals there before being promoted to the dining room.

Julia's little dog is lying asleep, apparently on a table, to the right of the picture, having kept Lili company once again while she worked.

THE KITCHEN 3 FEBRUARY 1847

IN JANUARY WILLIAM RALPH CARTWRIGHT DIED. OVERNIGHT, from being a foreign dependent, Lili found herself in the position of mistress of the house, as the wife of his heir, and the person who would supersede the much-loved Julia in this role. Julia would be expected, in the manner of that time, to live elsewhere. Lili felt isolated, foreign and alone while the others in the family drew together to deal with the great change. She feared they might resent her as an outsider and misunderstand her warmth towards them. As it took two weeks even

4 JANUARY 1847

Mr. Cart. died this morning at four-forty-five, without pain, without any effort or fighting; his death was so gentle that we hardly noticed it. . . . We are all bereaved with the loss which we have suffered, and amongst the servants, all over Aynhoe, tears are shed everywhere.

6 JANUARY 1847

The house is fuller than it has ever been; Stephen's house is also quite full. Stephen, together with William and Marianne, is making all the arrangements. I am trying to stay as far back as possible from the limelight and I would like to vanish if it were possible.

in good weather for letters to reach Stockholm and another two weeks to receive a reply, Sir Thomas was little help, and his next brother William acted, somewhat tactlessly, as his deputy. Lili's sense of alienation without her husband and elder son in the midst of these great changes became less oppressive as time went on, despite the vagaries of the postal system. She stayed as unobtrusive as possible while major decisions within the family were taken without reference to her. After a suitable time had elapsed, Lili returned to painting.

The great kitchen at Aynhoe was a good choice for her next painting, in view of the continuing cold weather. This important room was in the centre of the servants' wing and had unusually high windows facing towards the drying yard and the brewhouse to the west. When I knew it the kitchen was used as a store-room and it remained one until we left the house in 1960. When Lili painted her picture there were still many people coming and going, so the massive central table carries a variety of food in different stages of preparation. At the near end there is a splendid joint – possibly a leg of lamb – in a large square dish. Next to it are several woodcock, waiting to be plucked and dressed. Behind this lies a hare and a large bird which looks like a heron or a bittern. Neither would have been very palatable, or indeed ethical, as a quarry but they were not protected species at the time. They would all have been shot by the family or guests, and I suspect that Tommy may have accounted for the heron as he was inclined to shoot unusual birds, such as larks, when the mood took him.

Behind the mysterious bird there appears to be a terrine on a dish garnished with something like watercress and there are other dishes behind these. There are two large copper jugs on the table, one with a long spout. One of the kitchen maids is putting another jug on the table close by. She wears a sombre dress of flounced material with a spotless white apron and a white cap. Her companion, who I take to be that august personage, the cook, has a more substantial figure. She wears a dress of blue material sprigged with flowers. She seems to be preparing further dishes, one of them a pie, on another table by the window. She stands beside a row of lead-topped ovens which were probably fired by charcoal. In the corner is a low shelf covered in lead with a recess below. The great dresser by the door holds the copper cooking pans of different shapes and sizes. Most of these are still with us, although they are retired

13 JANUARY 1847

Alas, how could I make them understand the sisterly feelings which I have for all of them, when there must be so many things that they dislike in me. I often feel it impossible to fight all the prejudices attached to my being a stranger, and all the imperfections and the mistakes for which I have to be forgiven!

13 JANUARY 1847

I have received this morning a letter from Carl, dated the 29th; he is well, having fun and is happy to hear of his father's recovery. When I read these letters and look around me, and consider the change that has taken place here, and the sorrow which is felt everywhere as a result, I tremble at the thought of the effect that our last letters will have on this dear Carl.!

THE KITCHEN, 3 FEBRUARY 1847

11 JANUARY 1847

Our mourning clothes are being made in London, since all our maids are busy making their own. The whole house will be in mourning for a year as is customary, and the church remains draped with black during all that time. The cold weather has come back.

from use and are now purely ornamental. The china is mostly kitchenware, as one would expect, but there are also some large dishes for serving joints which would be suitable for taking into the dining room. There is a noble coffee grinder of cast iron between the dresser and the wall. Hanging from the ceiling is a brass or iron lamp, with its glass mantles, which must have given a poor light.

The large fireplace required cooking techniques far different from our own and would have been similar to those described in the early editions of Mrs Beeton. There are six cooking pots hanging from chains over it or sitting on top of the live coals supported by the front bars. The big chain is attached to the wall and the pots can be raised on it to the required height. In front stands the remarkable plate-warmer with its half-open doors showing the china ready for the dining room. It is on castors. When my mother first came to Aynhoe in the early 1930s the remains of this mobile cupboard were still in the kitchen, along with most of the other features shown in the painting. Behind the warming cupboard are two silvered plate-warmers for the sideboard. These would have been filled with hot coals or charcoal in the dining room. Beyond the fire was a second oven and there is a recess on the right-hand side which may have contained yet another. The door on the left led to the scullery and out of sight to the right was another doorway to a little room which was the cook's snuggery.

In the wall above are hatches for access to the chimney and the mechanism of the spit chain. There is a hatch in the ceiling, slightly ajar, which I take to be a ventilator. It looks as if the lever for opening it has been broken and the rope removed from the holder so that it has stuck in the position so carefully recorded by Lili.

The kitchen and its little adjoining room were successfully turned into a split-level flat after we left the house in 1960. I never knew this room, or any of the other ground-floor rooms of the west wing, when they were in use. There was a large amount of depressed-looking furniture in the kitchen throughout my childhood and it remained there until we left. However, my stepfather, Eustace Hoare, found there the missing section of a fine Georgian sideboard and several other forgotten items of importance and brought them back into use.

17 JANUARY 1847

I am having a difficult time; I am afraid to fail in many things, and make everything go wrong, which is one of the worst feelings one can have, when one wishes from the bottom of one's heart to reconcile everyone.

THE LAUNDRY   23 FEBRUARY 1847

20 JANUARY 1847

Charles Clerke told me today about Mr. Cart.'s Will, and explained the state of affairs. The future does not look very bright for dear Cart., and there is no doubt that during this year and even during next year, the income will pass into the hands of the Executors to pay for the funeral expenses, and share out the legacy and pensions, and unpaid accounts. The maintenance of the land and of the house is Cart.'s responsibility, and he will be forced to borrow considerable amounts of money...

IT SOON BECAME CLEAR THAT WILLIAM RALPH HAD LEFT SUCH large legacies to his family and servants that they would use up all the available cash and that it would take several years before the estate would be out of debt. Sir Thomas would have to continue as a diplomat in order to have any money at all, and now it would have to stretch to cover two households. Julia decided to live at Edgecott, a fine house a few miles away which belonged to the Carters, connections of the Aubrey family, and which was to be left to her son Richard Aubrey. Her departure, four weeks after her husband's death, made things less embarrassing for Lili, though she was sad to lose Julia's company, and she settled down to carry out the duties required of her as best she could.

Life proceeded quietly as she waited for Sir Thomas to return from Sweden, although the need to provide full mourning clothes for the entire household must have kept the female servants fully occupied with sewing, mending, washing, starching and ironing. Most of the family had dispersed to their own homes and she was left with Tommy and his tutor. She worried constantly about the financial trials that lay in store for her family, and she spent her mornings painting on her own.

At the end of the service wing was the laundry. Like the kitchen next door, it had three very high windows looking out on to the yard at the back. Outside these windows Lili shows a two-storey building which was originally the brewhouse. There exist two drawings by Nattes, who visited Aynhoe in 1815 and drew many pictures of the village and the house, which show the upper and lower floors of the brewhouse, full of vats and presses.

The laundry maids appear to be doing some ironing. I cannot make out if the objects in front of them are irons or not, since they appear to be of a different pattern from those being heated by the fire, or whether they are sprinklers used to keep the garments damp enough to iron. One of the laundry maids wears a grey dress with a modest pattern of flowers and the other has a plain dark grey dress. Both wear linen caps tied at the back

... All the silver, the linen, the carriages go to Mrs. Cart., who, besides her dower, will receive £2500. I am very glad to see that she is well provided for; she has been a very good mother for all of us, and it would be ungrateful of us to think otherwise. But there are pensions and legacies for the employees which are of too great a generosity; this proves that if Mr. Cart. had lived longer he would have been entirely governed by his servants. All these details have only been sent to Cart. last Monday, and will perhaps arrive too late to avoid his departure. I tremble at the thought of the effect that this news will have on him. I am very worried about all this, and I feel more than ever – and this has been the turning point of my life – my excessive poverty, which prevents me from helping him, other than praying the Lord to grant him wisdom, caution and courage, to envisage the difficulties of the moment, and find ways to solve them. I pray the Lord to answer this prayer, and help my poor husband.

Wash drawing of the interior of the Aynhoe brewhouse by Nattes, where beer for the household was brewed.

with ribbons. Close to them lie two baskets of clothes which seem to be the next group to be ironed. To their left, and below the small mirror, are two small baskets with central posts, perhaps for shaping lace caps and allowing them to dry before ironing without being crushed. Further along the bench is a big draining board, a basket and an object which may be a brush. Under the bench, which is used as an ironing board, is a collection of useful jugs, boxes and coppers. There are four more big laundry baskets, three of them hanging on the wall.

On the left-hand side of the picture is the large clothes press for squeezing water from the washing – something of a contrast in style to our own tumble-drier. Ted Humphris, our head gardener for many years, remembers that it was one of his first jobs as the garden boy to work this machine once a week, and very temperamental it was. Up on the ceiling hangs the huge drying rack. Not in use at the moment, it has been pulled up out of the way by a pulley which is out of the picture. The frame is wooden but the bars appear to be made of rope. This is a most useful gadget of a type which has been in use since time immemorial and which is still available in a more modest size via the mail order catalogues.

To the right is the fireplace with a large clothes horse in front of it. A variety of white wear hangs on it, with various items trimmed with red and with a little cap of lace at the top. At the extreme right there is a blue dress hanging in front of what appears to be a flue. Perhaps its design, in front of the wall, enabled a mild warmth to be given to delicate materials away from the fire. I cannot figure out the purpose of the steps shown below. Several of the shutters on the windows are partly open. It is my guess that the steamy atmosphere of the laundry caused them to warp so that they could no longer be folded back into their panelled recesses.

23 FEBRUARY 1847

The day was a happy one for me, for it brought two letters from Cart., the one of the 2nd and the other of the 9th of February. He tells me that he will be here in the first days of May, and what reassures me about our future is that he is not discouraged by the sad state of these pecuniary affairs and that he hopes to be able to deal with them with wisdom and prudence. He is not thinking of abandoning his diplomatic career which is a great help in view of the circumstances.

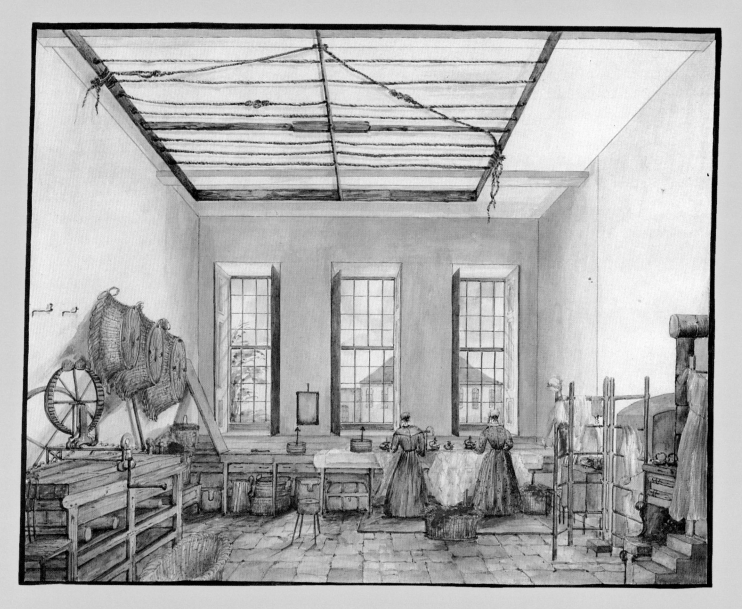

THE LAUNDRY, 23 FEBRUARY 1847

THE SERVANTS' HALL   20 MARCH 1847

24 MARCH 1847

The day of fasting which was ordered by the Queen and the Government for the whole of Great Britain took place today. It was ordered to obtain from God the end of famine and the calamities which weigh down poor Ireland. After lunch, I went to our Chapel in Banbury . . .

THE BITTERLY COLD WINTER HAD CAUSED MUCH HARDSHIP IN the village. Lili and Stephen organized soup kitchens in the village on Tuesdays and Thursdays, each of them looking after half of the village. This was soon to be followed by the distribution of blankets and, rather oddly, quantities of rice, which was more readily available at the time than corn. Sir Thomas, by letter, had put Lili in charge of the running of the gardens, the poultry at the home farm and the governing of the school, so that she was now considerably busier. Despite this, she always retained her lively interest in international affairs, unlike so many of the English squirearchy and their ladies with their parochial attitudes. The Irish potato famine to which she referred in the autumn and now once again in March had reached such proportions that the Government could no longer ignore it. It was eventually to reduce the population of Ireland by nearly a third. However, her pious sentiments on behalf of the Irish do not seem to have caused her to abandon her lunch altogether.

After her visit to Great Tew Lili could hardly conceal her satisfaction at finding the results of Mr Boulton's excessively expensive building work to be so tasteless. I confess that we shared her views when we would go there for tea. We used to refer to the house as 'Nightmare Abbey'. To judge from her comments about the housekeeper, Lili was now having difficulties not only with the family but also with the staff at Aynhoe.

In the service wing, but facing the main courtyard, the servants' hall could seat a large number, and it needed to do so. Here the staff had their meals, sitting at the long central table on the benches. The table between the windows looks as if it could be extended by using the leaves on top should there be many visiting servants in the house. These could be a considerable number since most people would bring a valet or a maid. Even in the 1930s my parents were expected to bring a valet and a

12 MARCH 1847

After finishing our correspondence for Stockholm, we went over to Tew to see the progress of the house. It is and will remain an ugly house and it seems even more cramped and miserable now that it is attached to the Gothick library which Mr. Boulton has had built, which has cost him an enormous amount. It does not blend with the rest and in any case has some architectural faults and errors of good taste which leaped to my eyes. The best thing about Tew is the housekeeper; I wish I could have such a one in my service.

24 MARCH 1847

The gardener discovered today that the potatoes in our potato patch have been attacked by the disease which is destroying all the potato fields, and he is very upset. The potatoes around Aynhoe are still healthy. May God grant us a fine crop of everything that is necessary for the poor people. We have established the distribution of rice here which will last until the end of the season.

lady's maid when they stayed at Castle Ashby or other great houses for shooting parties.

The room is sparsely furnished, with only a curious folding rack and a fine long-case clock in addition to the tables. The clock has the phases of the moon above the dial and is still with us. The basket for cutlery stands on the table and there is a cupboard at the far end for china. The sunshine of late morning streams in through the windows.

There is an intriguing collection of fire-fighting equipment hanging from the two beams, including fifteen buckets, probably made of leather. We still have some, rescued from the loft above the garage, but they appear to be of a different shape and therefore may come from another set. Below these, on the second beam, hang the gauntlets of heavy leather and next to them a leather helmet and two pairs of thigh boots. Fire-fighting kit was as important then as it is now, although at that time it was pathetically unlikely that any major fire could be conquered using the horse-drawn estate fire engine and the fire buckets. Consequently, many great houses burned down.

By the door of the servants' hall is a coat rack with pegs and above hangs the first of the five pictures. Unfortunately none of these can be identified, but they look as if they are family portraits; no doubt these would be of the more obscure, badly painted or unpopular family members from previous generations or they would have been promoted to a more prominent position in the house. Perhaps the two religious paintings have been hung there to encourage a high moral tone during mealtime discussions.

Ink drawing by Lili of the sledge in which Sir Thomas journeyed to Christiania in Norway on diplomatic business during the winter. Sent in a letter to Julia and put into her scrapbook.

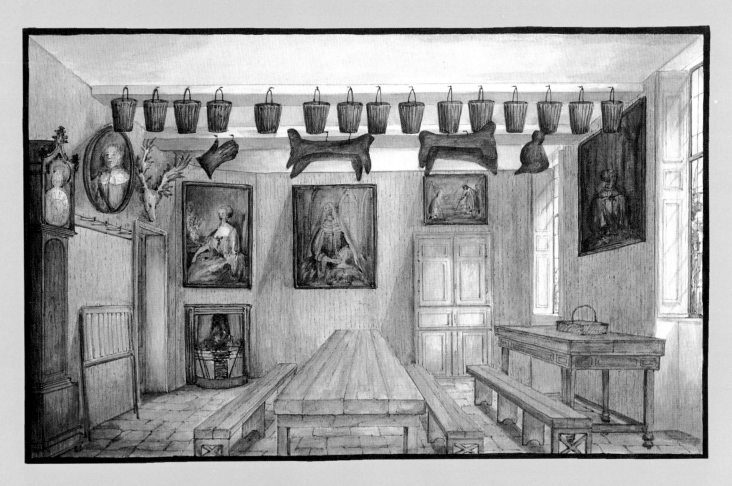

THE SERVANTS' HALL, 20 MARCH 1847

THE COLD BATH ROOM, 8 MAY 1847

THE COLD BATH ROOM   8 MAY 1847

AS SO OFTEN IN THE PAST, AFFAIRS OF STATE – ON THIS occasion the forthcoming coronation of the King of Norway which Sir Thomas, as British Minister, was obliged to attend – were to determine when Lili would next see her husband. Having devoted the winter to carrying out all her new duties, while struggling against ill-health, anxiety and the suggestion of lack of cooperation from some members of the family, she now resigned herself to spending a cold, wet English summer without him. The 'stomach-strengthening' medicine prescribed by her physician seems not to have helped very much. She spent much of her time wrapped up by the fire in her room and drawing. Mercifully, she was not tempted to test the therapeutic qualities of the cold bath.

When Sir John Soane remodelled most of the interior of the house he put in this extraordinary room next to the orangery. A similar cold bath existed at nearby Rousham. It may have been inspired by the many visits to Bath by William Ralph and his family at the end of the eighteenth and the beginning of the nineteenth century. There were several spas in the area, notably Astrop Spa with its chalybeate springs, where bathing in the mineral waters as well as drinking them was considered therapeutic. Aynho, too, had at least one chalybeate spring, which was highly regarded even though it was never exploited commercially. From the eighteenth century until our own day the water supply to the house was pumped up from the spring at the cottage on the Banbury road opposite College Farm, which until recently was occupied by Laurence Cole, who had been the agent. The water was held in large tanks on the roof of the park house. No doubt there had originally been wells closer to the house as there are a number of wells visible in the drawings of the village made by Nattes in 1815. The brewhouse behind the west wing certainly would have had its own well.

5 MAY 1847

I have been ill and in pain during the whole night, but having arranged a visit to Sir John Clerke, I said nothing, and I went to see him in London. . . . Sir John Clerke gave me once again some stomach-strengthening medicine which I hope will give me back my health.

Unfinished pencil sketch by Lili, 1847, of Tommy, Mr. Algar and Lucy in the Salon at Aynhoe during the period after William Ralph's death.

The cold bath is about six feet deep, with steps curving down into it. The water pipe emerges from one of the pillars, which was perhaps designed to conceal the source. The interior of the bath is tiled. It all looks extremely forbidding and it must have required much fortitude to use it. Hot baths in the nineteenth century were obtainable in the bedrooms and through the use of hip baths. These were brought in by the menservants and filled with hot water from buckets by some unfortunate maidservant, who had to struggle up the stairs with them from the remote fastness of the kitchen. My parents introduced several baths on the main floors in the 1930s. When I knew the house the Army had bequeathed us a number of Sadia water heaters which provided two inches of boiling water, full of limescale and brown stain, and thereafter tended to explode, so that it was necessary to supervise them very carefully. Also there were no bathroom heaters and the floors were covered in mouse-nibbled linoleum, which made bathing a rather spartan affair.

The cold bath had not been in use for many years, and before the house was opened to the public my father built on a room beyond the arched window shown in the painting to house his collection of Chinese porcelain, displayed in elegantly arched cabinets made of hardboard. The bath was concreted in as it would have been a most effective visitor-trap, but the outline still shows in the floor. These two rooms are now used as the kitchens of the Country Households.

Water from the cold bath would have joined the main drains in some mysterious fashion. When we were leaving Aynhoe it was necessary to discover the external drainage plan. The only man who knew where the drains went was an old man in the village who was determined that the secret should die with him. As he refused to divulge the information, we were treated to the sight of the estate agents digging for them in the lawn. Eventually the main chamber was found, halfway down the park.

8 MAY 1847

This morning I received a very long letter from Cart. of the 27th. The Coronation is not yet fixed, and the doubts about this subject are being covered up because in Norway, as almost everywhere else, the lack of grain is afflicting the country. The King wants to see his Coronation put off until a more fertile and more favourable year. The Coronation (if it takes place) will only be in July and if Cart. must be there, he will not be here until August. The rain only stopped for short intervals.

[119]

THE OAK STAIRCASE, 7 JUNE 1847

THE OAK STAIRCASE, 11 JUNE 1847

THE OAK STAIRCASE   7 AND 11 JUNE 1847

L ILI HAD SPENT MOST OF MAY IN LONDON WHERE SHE WENT TO obtain treatment for her illness. The sophisticated social life she found there must have presented a great contrast to the rather solitary and dutiful existence she led at Aynhoe, although she seemed glad to return and was taking more interest in Tommy's activities in between lessons with his tutor, Mr Algar. Before leaving London she had received letters from both Sir Thomas and Willy. Her return to Aynhoe was made more pleasurable by the prospect of being joined by them both before the end of the summer. She therefore settled contentedly to document the few remaining corners of the main house, now so familiar to her, which she had not yet painted.

When Soane remodelled the space around the staircase with columns and a domed ceiling he left the stairs themselves unchanged, and these date from around 1707. The balusters are all carved and are most attractive. Lili's paintings show the area much the same as it was when I knew it, although we had much more furniture at the bottom since it was part of the house which was open to the public. In the painting of the upper part of the staircase Lili seems to have taken more trouble, perhaps enjoying a sense of mastery of the rather difficult perspective. She shows the view through the windows, looking out over the main courtyard towards the north. This is now an open area of lawn, but in 1847 it was full of trees screening the house from the road through the village. The circular lawn in the courtyard and the curved wall remain as they were then.

The treads of the staircase are of wood inlaid with patterns which show more clearly in the painting than they do now. There is a woolly red rug at the top, no doubt joining the stairway to the corridor carpet. As children we had our bedrooms directly at the top of this staircase and it was a convenient short cut to the hall and to the outside world.

29 MAY 1847

I saw Mathilde, who came at five o'clock to take me for a carriage drive in the park. It was full of people and we met the Queen and her children twice. London is very brilliant; the Grand-Duke Constantin of Russia, the Hereditary Grand Duke and the Grand-Duchess of Saxe-Weimar and the Prince of Lugues are here. They are being fêted at the Court and Mathilde, who is in waiting there, has few moments to give me. I will dine with her next Monday if she is not obliged to take herself to Windsor where the Queen and the foreign princes will be spending the week at Ascot races.

31 MAY 1847

I made some visits with Mathilde and many purchases and then dined with her, and after that we rejoined Mme. Rethausen in her box at the French Theatre where we saw Les Demoiselles de St. Cyr and Les Précieuses Ridicules. I did not return until midnight, a very late hour for me.

2 JUNE 1847

Before leaving London, I received with pleasure a letter from Willy. He is on the point of leaving Rome and setting off for Civita Vecchia to go to Genoa and from there to Geneva. . . . The countryside is superb and my heart beat with joy to find myself there again and to see Aynhoe in all its beauty. After dinner I settled myself in the garden where I breathed fine and good fresh air which did me much good.

However, for quite a long time we were unable to use them. There was dry rot which was spreading enthusiastically from the ancient cellar below and the entire floor below the stairs and the passage had to be taken up, as well as the first flight of the stairs themselves. This meant that the stairs ended halfway down above a black pit more than twenty feet deep, and a barrier of string was put across them on which hung a skull and crossbones. It all looked very sinister at night. Eventually, the wooden boards were replaced by concrete after a second outbreak of dry rot, and the original stair treads were returned to their places, happily unaffected.

The portrait on the left is of a Lady Howard (we have not yet discovered which Lady Howard, since there were many). Lili has written 'Lady H' in minute lettering in the correct place upon it. This picture always intrigued us since we can find no connection between her and the Cartwright family which would explain her presence at Aynhoe, and why she should be holding a letter from Lord Chandos and looking very mournful. On the right-hand side of the staircase is an unidentifiable portrait, and it is thought that the one on the left is of Armine Cartwright by Hudson. She was the daughter of Thomas Cartwright, who extended the house around 1707, and she married William Ward. For some reason they lived for many years in a flat on the top floor of the house, where they wrote letters complaining about the way Thomas treated them and how pompous he had become.

This is the last of Lili's paintings of the interior of the house, although she did preliminary sketches for a painting of the white staircase by Soane at the other end of the main house. Forbidden to run on the oak stairs as the treads creaked alarmingly and it was very slippery, as children we could, and did, slide down the banisters of the white stairs from top to bottom on the way down to lunch.

Afterword

Cartoon of Willy (William Cornwallis Cartwright) as Member of Parliament for Oxfordshire in the 1860s, by Spy. He stood first as a Liberal, against the traditions of the family, but became a Tory on the issue of Home Rule for Ireland.

L
ILI'S STAY AT AYNHOE ENDED ON A HAPPY NOTE, REUNITED AS she was at last with all her family. Sir Thomas had returned to England to sort out the more pressing financial problems of the estate, which eventually proved intractable. He had in any case inherited his father's inability to economize. He and Lili continued to rely on his income as British Minister in Sweden to support them all, and so were obliged to return to Stockholm a few months later. From there, he kept up a copious correspondence with his brother William over the running of the estate and the introduction of the improved farming methods that he wished to see. Only three years after Lili's last painting of Aynhoe, in 1850, Sir Thomas died, worn out by the double burden of his financial problems and his diplomatic duties.

Further distress was added to Lili's situation when Willy announced that he had got married. He had been roaming about Europe with little notion of the financial problems besetting his parents, and more interested in the political and revolutionary movements in all the countries he visited. On his travels he met Clementine Gaul, who was travelling as the companion of a Russian lady. Clementine was the natural daughter of a Russian prince, the aide-de-camp of Grand Duke Constantine, and of a daughter of the Remorsky family, exiled from Poland. She was already pregnant but not, it seems, by Willy. Her daughter Wanda was born soon afterwards. As they had married in Breslau, and were without papers and unable to find evidence of their marriage, they remarried in Cairo in 1850. Lili was appalled at Willy's marriage to a woman she described as 'an unworthy person' and never fully forgave her son.

17 JULY 1847

Today was a happy one and should be marked in red: Cart. and Willy arrived and so we are all reunited, through the goodness of God, who I thank for this grace. . . . All the household has arrived and our three foreign servants, speaking only their own language, must be making the Housekeeper's room and the Servants' Hall a little tower of Babel.

So great were the debts attached to the estate that Willy let the house for almost the rest of the century, and he and Clementine lived mostly in Florence and Rome. Despite his lack of an Oxford education he became something of an intellectual. He travelled widely, became a highly respected correspondent for *The Times*, wrote a number of books and articles, and reported to the British Government on political and social issues in the new united Italy. So great was his expertise in the end, and so wide was his acquaintance (including the great figures of the Risorgimento and leading British artists and intellectuals such as Robert Browning and Lord Leighton) that Gladstone called him 'the longest head in Europe' when it came to foreign affairs. In the 1860s he returned to Aynho to become the Liberal MP for Oxfordshire (other members of the family having tied up South Northamptonshire for the Tories) and, as we already know, lived in one of the cottages painted by Lili. His marriage to Clementine was not altogether successful, it seems, but they stayed together until she died in 1890. Willy only returned to live at Aynhoe at the end of the century, when his nephew Fairfax, the son of William and Marianne, left him enough money from his mother's London estate to enable him to do so.

William and Marianne continued to rent Flore House near Northampton. William was told, rather brusquely, to stop interfering with matters concerning the estate by Willy, the new heir, and thereafter turned his attention to other things. He became one of the first Commissioners of Police and concerned himself with local affairs. He rescued two ladies from drowning when they had fallen into a river – an act of bravery that might have been expected from a man who had fought at the Peninsular War and at Waterloo so many years before.

Lili retired to Leamington Spa soon after Willy inherited Aynhoe. We are not sure why she chose Leamington, although several of the family lived in the area and the new railway from there made visits to them much easier. She also had the advantage of being able to visit the Catholic church there whenever she wished. She resided there for fifty-two years until she died, aged ninety-seven, in 1902. Any further paintings she may have made have not survived within the family, but she kept up her diary until the day she died.

Tommy, ever dependable, married the heiress of the Leslie-Melville family of Melville in Fife. One of his daughters married a Cottrell-

Pencil portrait of Col. William Cartwright by his brother-in-law, Matthew Boulton. From Julia's scrapbook.

Dormer of Rousham in Oxfordshire, a family to which the Cartwrights were already distantly related. Lili left her paintings, her diary and her remarkable collection of Continental porcelain to this granddaughter. Thomas Cottrell-Dormer, her son, gave the paintings and some of the diary to my mother as they referred mostly to Aynhoe, and I am deeply indebted to him for this and for his help. Some months ago he reminded me that he remembers Lili quite clearly, as he and his brothers used to stay with her in Leamington on their train journeys in the holidays from Melville, before taking the local train on to Rousham. He recalls her as a tiny, kindly old lady with a strong German accent, alert and spry, who took much interest in the boys and gave them beautiful hand-made toys from Germany. It is a remarkable memory; she was, after all, born ten years before the battle of Waterloo.

Portrait of Lili in her mourning clothes. Drawn by A. Greaffle, about 1850.

Acknowledgements

I would like to express my gratitude to the following people for their invaluable help in the preparation of this book:

To Thomas Cottrell-Dormer for giving my mother the early diaries and the paintings and for his recollections of Lili and of his visits to Sandizell.

To his son, Charles Cottrell-Dormer, for the loan of the diary covering the period of the death of William Ralph Cartwright and the years immediately following this.

To Fred and Sally Cartwright for the loan of the scrapbooks from which so many illustrations have been taken.

To my husband and son for putting up with my preoccupation with the typewriter and the nineteenth century and for my husband's helpful criticism.

To Fionnoula Coulson and Angela Beloe for typing endless pieces of manuscript without flinching.

To Barbara Ford for managing to read Lili's defensive handwriting and for translating a large part of the second half of the diary used in this book.

To Jeremy Maas for his enthusiasm for Lili's pictures and his help in getting the book published.

To Michael Voggenaur for his researches in Bavaria.

To Peter Thornton for his kindness in allowing me to examine Sir John Soane's plans of Aynhoe in the Soane Museum.

Bibliography

COOPER, NICHOLAS, *Aynho: A Northamptonshire Village*. Leopard's Head Press in conjunction with Banbury Historical Society, Volume 20, 1984.

DAVIDSON, CAROLINE, *The World of Mary Ellen Best*. Chatto and Windus, The Hogarth Press, London, 1985.

FORRESTER, ERIC G., *Northampton County Elections and Electioneering, 1695–1832*. Oxford University Press, London: Humphrey Milford, 1941.

GIROUARD, MARK, *Life in the English Country House*. Yale University Press, New Haven and London, 1978.

HUMPHRIS, TED, *Garden Glory*. Collins, reprinted 1988.

THORNTON, PETER, *Authentic Decor; The Domestic Interior. 1620–1920*. Weidenfeld and Nicolson, London, 1984.

Victoria County History. *Northamptonshire Families*. ed. Oswald Barron F.S.A. Archibald Constable and Co. London. 1906.

Index